GETTYSBURG

and the Christian Commission

George H. Stuart
Chairman of the United States Christian Commission

GETTYSBURG

and the Christian Commission

Daniel John Hoisington

Edinborough Press

Edinborough Press
1-888-251-6336
www.edinborough.com
books@edinborough.com

Pejepscot Historical Society
159 Park Row
Brunswick, Maine 04011

The text is composed in Wessex and printed on acid free paper.
Research Associate: Daniel Aaron Hoisington

Library of Congress Cataloging-in-Publication Data
Gettysburg and the Christian Commission / [edited by] Daniel John Hoisington.
   p.   cm.
   Includes bibliographical references.
   ISBN 1-889020-05-2 (alk. paper)
   1. Gettysburg, Battle of, Gettysburg, Pa., 1863. 2. United States Christian Commission. 3. United States–History–Civil War, 1861-1865–Religious aspects. 4. United States–History–Civil War, 1861-1865–Medical care. 5. United States–History–Civil War, 1861-1865–Civilian relief. 6. Gettysburg, Battle of, Gettysburg, Pa., 1863–Sources. 7. Gettysburg, Battle of, Gettysburg, Pa., 1863–Personal narratives. I. Hoisington, Daniel John.
   E475.53 .G3936 2002
   973.7'349--dc21
   2002007655

Contents

✝ ✝ ✝ ✝ ✝ ✝ ✝

Preface

A Thousand Nameless Acts
Daniel John Hoisington
I

The Battle of Gettysburg and the Christian Commission
Andrew Boyd Cross
39

A Delegate's Diary
John Calhoun Chamberlain
73

An Incident at Gettysburg
Jane Boswell Moore
105

Two Brass Buttons
George Alexander Peltz
121

John Schick Store
ADAMS COUNTY HISTORICAL SOCIETY
GETTYSBURG, PENNSYLVANIA

Martin Stoever, with the white beard, stands in the doorway. Stoever, a professor at Gettysburg College, owned the building and lived next door. John L. Schick's store was used by the Christian Commission as a warehouse after the battle of Gettysburg.

Preface

After September 11, 2001, America witnessed a tremendous outpouring of aid to the victims of the destruction of the World Trade Center. Step back, then, to the year 1863 and consider the impact of the battle of Gettysburg. Three days of conflict left 7,000 dead and 26,000 wounded soldiers within a day's journey from all major Eastern cities, including New York, Philadelphia, Boston, and Pittsburgh. This book tells the story of the response of one relief agency, the United States Christian Commission.

Despite its importance to the northern war effort, many historians fail to understand the work of the Commission. One influential collection of essays, *Religion and the American Civil War*, has only two minor references to the organization. A standard college-level text, *The Civil War and Reconstruction*, written by three preeminent scholars, described the Commission as "organized and run by the 'relief ladies'." Allen Guelzo, in his recent *Abraham Lincoln: Redeemer President*, incorrectly stated, "Northern Democrat elites shuddered with contempt when the United States Christian Commission organized 5,000 agents to travel with the federal armies, distributing religious tracts and preaching abolition, and they organized a rival United States Sanitary Commission."

This collection, a prelude to a complete history of the organization, will hopefully restore the Commission to the importance given it by contemporaries. In my research, many fine historians and archivists assisted me, including Theresa McDevitt, Steve Zerbe, the Adams County Historical Society, and the Special Collections Department of the Bowdoin College Library. The Pejepscot Historical Society granted permission to publish the complete Christian Commission journal of John C. Chamberlain. Paul Downing gave a careful reading to the transcription of the journal and made several key corrections. Thanks also go to the Huntington Library, Presbyterian Historical Society, Lutheran Seminary, Bethel Seminary, Minnesota Historical Society, Massachusetts Historical Society, and the American Antiquarian Society. Larry McGrane, a Christian gentleman and dedicated Civil War re-enactor, was especially invaluable.

Finally, I dedicate this book to my brother, R. Michael Hoisington. Like the men and women of the Christian Commission, he has traveled to "the front" in God's service. ☩

Second Corps Hospital

THE PHOTOGRAPHIC HISTORY OF THE CIVIL WAR

William Frassanito concludes that Frederick Gutekunst took this photograph in the Second Corps Hospital around July 9 and 10. The two men on the left appear to wear the distinctive pin of the United States Christian Commission.

"A Thousand Nameless Acts"
The Christian Commission at Gettysburg

✢ ✢ ✢ ✢ ✢ ✢ ✢

Daniel John Hoisington

R OBERT McCREARY stood on his rooftop, observing a battle unfold on the
streets of his hometown of Gettysburg. Glancing at nearby houses, he
watched his neighbors cheering on advances by the Union army. Soon, the
distant boom of cannon fire rose to a crescendo as the fighting came closer.
On the streets below, McCreary saw soldiers carrying litters of wounded
men, desperately searching for a safe haven. He wrote,

> Descending from my chimney-top, and gathering up a basket of band-
> ages, with basin, sponge, scissors, and pins, I hastened to the nearest
> hospital, which I found in a warehouse about two hundred yards from
> my residence.[1]

During the month of June, Jonathan Edwards Adams, a thirty-five-
year-old minister from New Sharon, Maine, worked as a delegate of the
United States Christian Commission in military camps around Alexandria,
Virginia. When the Army of the Potomac moved north, following the
Confederate advance into Pennsylvania, Adams traveled to Washington to
call on patients in nearby hospitals. Far from home, he visited the national
shrines, touring the Smithsonian Institution, the White House, and the
Capitol. On Friday, July 3, as word spread of the great battle, Adams rushed
to the railroad station, catching a train to Westminster, Maryland, where the
Western Maryland Railroad ended. Still twenty-five miles from Gettysburg,

---

[1] United States Christian Commission for the Army and Navy, *Second Annual Report
for the Year 1863* (Philadelphia: James B. Rogers, 1864), 61. Hereafter cited as USCC,
Second Annual Report.

I

he climbed on a wagon headed north, arriving on the battlefield late on July 4. That evening, he wrote, "Rolled over to the scene of battle—awful! Bringing in wounded all day. Saw and helped in amputations." Within days, the Commission placed Adams in charge of the Third Division, Second Corps Hospital, where he remained for three weeks.[2]

When Clarissa Jones, a Philadelphia schoolteacher, learned of the battle, she convinced several local druggists to donate medicine. After carefully packing the supplies into eight barrels, she marched down to the national headquarters of the Christian Commission. When she offered her services to George Stuart, the chairman, he proved reluctant to accept a female delegate. Instead, Stuart suggested that she go to Baltimore, knowing that their branch office often sent women to the front. Jones took the train to Baltimore, then, with an official letter in hand, on to Gettysburg. The army, however, confiscated her barrels when rumors spread that a Mrs. C. F. Jones, a Southern sympathizer, was aiding Rebel soldiers. Meeting with military authorities, Jones convinced them that she was not a rebel spy, and then went to work in the Second Corps hospital.[3]

On July 3 Charles Keener, superintendent of the Maryland Institution for the Blind, was escorting two young students to their homes in Frederick when he learned of the battle. He set out on foot for Gettysburg, wandering through the night until, exhausted, he fell asleep on the ground. The next morning, as he approached Emmitsburg, a heavy storm struck. He wrote, "I waded through mountain torrents of rain-water, over knee deep, and so swift that I expected momentarily to be swept before the dashing current." As he waited out the storm in town, Confederate cavalry rode through on their retreat. Finally, on July 5, Keener joined an Army photographer, "quite adroit in escaping from the Rebs," headed for Gettysburg. He finally arrived on Sunday evening.[4]

---

[2] Jonathan E. Adams Diary, Special Collections, Bowdoin College Library, Brunswick, Maine; William Cushing Adams, *Jonathan Edwards Adams, D.D., and Maine Congregationalism* (Portland, Maine: Southworth Press, 1933).

[3] Clarissa Fellows Jones, Pension file, 5 February 1917, National Archives and Record Administration; *Philadelphia North American*, 29 June 1913, special section, 4.

[4] United States Christian Commission, *Second Report of the Committee of Maryland* (Baltimore: James Young, 1864), 88-91. Hereafter cited as Maryland Committee, *Second Annual Report*.

While these men and women took different roads to Gettysburg, the United States Christian Commission brought them together in common cause over the coming weeks.

The Roots of the Christian Commission

On the eve of the Civil War, the Young Men's Christian Association (YMCA) was, as one contemporary described it, a "wide-spreading league of Christian youth." Founded in the United States in 1851, the Association established local chapters in many major cities and college campuses. It appealed to students and young urban workers, offering a Christian identity without the ecclesiastical responsibilities of the institutional church. In the eyes of evangelical leaders, it provided a safe haven for impressionable men, away from family influence and easily enticed by the camaraderie of saloons and gambling halls. However, the organization's growth stagnated after 1856.[5]

A wave of religious enthusiasm, known as the Great Revival, swept through the major Northern cities during the winter of 1857-58, re-energizing the YMCA in its wake. As one observer wrote, "The public interest was unprecedented. The entire nation seemed to be the scene of one vast revival." The Baltimore Association held nine daily meetings during the height of the revival. In Philadelphia, thousands gathered in churches and firehouses. Boston's meetings were "crowded to excess." Two thousand people attended meetings in Cleveland. A YMCA historian wrote, "Without [the revival] the Movement might have dwindled out during the Civil War, for it was definitely on the decline in 1857."[6]

Revival leaders adopted worship practices that greatly influenced the Christian Commission. The heart of the awakening lay in its weekday noon meetings rather than in Sunday morning church services. These "business men's meetings" featured scripture reading and hymns, followed by prayers and testimonies from the audience. Carefully avoiding theological pitfalls, politics, and denominationalism, signs hung in the front of meetings that reminded speakers, "No controverted points discussed." Laymen, rather than ordained clergy, directed the meetings. Samuel Iranaeus Prime wrote,

[5] Richard Morse, *History of the North American Young Men's Christian Associations* (New York: Association Press, 1913), 14-17; C. Howard Hopkins, *History of the Y.M.C.A. in North* America (New York: Association Press, 1951), 54-98.

[6] Hopkins, *History of the Y.M.C.A.*, 54-98.

"Clergymen share in the conduct [of the noon meetings], but no more than laymen, and as much as if they were laymen."[7]

The revival awakened a hope that the church might reclaim "manly" attitudes after being relegated to the "women's sphere" in antebellum culture. The *Christian Advocate and Journal* stated that the revival "prevails chiefly among a class of men who are usually the least affected by revivals—the practical business men of the cities." In turn, the entrepreneurial attitude shaped spiritual expression. Talbot Chambers wrote, "There is a promptness, an earnestness, a directness, which allow no dragging, and show that men have come together for a purpose, and mean, with God's blessing, to accomplish that purpose."[8]

It furnished a generation of men who, if not social reformers, were activists in their interaction with society. They responded to the call of Dudley Tyng, a dynamic young Philadelphia minister, when he preached to a noon businessmen's meeting on Exodus 10:11, "Go now ye that are men and serve the Lord." After the young preacher's tragic death, just weeks later, they sang the powerful words of George Duffield's 1858 hymn, based on Tyng's last words, "Stand up! Stand up for Jesus! Ye soldiers of the cross!"

Examples abound of the links between the spiritual inspiration of the 1857 Revival and the Christian Commission. In Chicago, Presbyterian layman J. B. Stillson spent his free hours wandering through the docks on Lake Michigan, handing out tracts and preaching on street corners, where he met a young shoe salesman named Dwight Moody. After mentoring the younger man, Stillson helped Moody organize a Sunday School in the city's poorest neighborhood. Similarly, Charles Keener, moved by a religious awakening during the revival, went to work in the Five Points slums of New York City. Duffield, Stillson, and Keener all served with the United States Christian Commission at Gettysburg.[9]

---

[7] Samuel Iranaeus Prime, *The Power of Prayer, Illustrated in the Wonderful Displays of Divine Grace at the Fulton Street and Other Meetings* (New York: Scribner, 1858) 57. See Kathryn Long, *The Revival of 1857-58: Interpreting an American Religious Awakening* (New York: Oxford University Press, 1998).

[8] *Christian Advocate and Journal*, 11 March 1858; Talbot Chambers, *The Noon Prayer Meeting of the North Dutch Church* (New York: Board of Publication, Reformed Protestant Dutch Church, 1858), 57.

Following the attack on Fort Sumter in April 1861, when President Lincoln issued a call for a volunteer army to suppress the rebellion, the young men who formed the core of the YMCA marched off to war. In the early days of mobilization, local branches sent representatives to visit troops as they gathered at mustering points just outside the large cities. When the soldiers marched south, they followed. A New York City leader, Vincent Colyer, traveled to Washington, D. C. to work among the camps that circled the capital, and became frustrated by the lack of coordination between the various city branches. Following the battle of Bull Run, he lobbied for a new, independent national organization. In response, YMCA leaders met in New York in November 1861 and formed the United States Christian Commission.[10]

This Convention chose George H. Stuart, chairman of the YMCA, as the new organization's leader. Stuart combined a nearly perfect blend of sound business judgment with a deep spiritual commitment. Born in Ulster, he came to America as a young man and worked at his brothers' import firm. Although a wealthy and successful businessman, by the 1850s, he increasingly turned his interests to Christian service. A contemporary credited the success of the Commission to Stuart's "wonderful administrative ability, his powerful influence with business men, and his magnetic style of oratory."[11]

During its first year, the Commission focused on spiritual needs and spent most of its budget on the distribution of Bibles, tracts, and religious periodicals. The public response was tepid, as the official history noted, "The Christian Commission seems at first to have been regarded by the public, not with distrust, for there was hardly interest enough manifested to warrant the ascription of such a feeling, but with general indifference." By late 1862, the organization had raised only $40,000 and church leaders largely ignored the Commission. General Secretary Archibald Morrison wrote that the work allowed ample time for prayer. The problem, he told

[9] Moody played an important role in the Chicago branch of the Christian Commission. Lyle Dorsett, *A Passion for Souls: The Life of D. L. Moody* (Chicago: Moody Press, 1997), 62-66; James F. Findlay Jr., *Dwight L. Moody: An American Evangelist, 1837-1899* (Chicago: University of Chicago Press, 1969), 76.

[10] Cephas Brainerd, *Christian Work in the Army prior to the Organization of the United States Christian Commission* (New York: John Medole, 1866).

[11] James Grant, *The Flag and the Cross: A History of the United States Christian Commission* (typescript, Historical Society of Pennsylvania, dated 1894), 12.

Stuart, was a "great confusion in the public mind…among the numerous agencies busied in similar operations."[12]

The Commission lay dormant until its leaders made several crucial changes that transformed the organization. In late summer of 1862, Stuart stepped into an active management role, receiving authority from the executive board to make important decisions with substantial independence. Then, in January 1863, Stuart moved the national headquarters from New York City to Philadelphia, providing office and warehouse space in his company's Bank Street building.

At the same time, Stuart changed the day-to-day management, hiring William Boardman as General Secretary in August 1862. Boardman brought experience to the position, having worked for the American Sunday School Union. As director of its Students' Mission Service, he managed an outreach program that sent more than three hundred theological students into the field each summer. A best-selling author, Boardman's call to piety, *A Higher Christian Life*, sold more than one hundred thousand copies during the height of the Great Revival.[13]

To dispel the public's "general indifference," the USCC needed to sharply distinguish its mission from similar organizations. Although myriad civilian relief agencies sprang up across the North in the first year of the war, the United States Sanitary Commission (USSC) was the dominant organization. Its influence had greatly improved conditions in the camps and provided much needed medical supplies to the Army. Through its subordinate Women's Central Association for Relief (WCAR), thousands of small local soldiers' aid societies gathered goods to ship to the front.

The Sanitary Commission, headed by Unitarian minister Henry Bellows, embraced a philosophy of disinterested benevolence. This view expressed a desire to separate personal piety and religious belief from social reform. Its first *Bulletin* stated, "Only the most persistent and strenuous resistance to an impulsive benevolence, the most earnest and obstinate defence of a guarded and methodized system of relief, can save the public from imposition,

---

[12] Lemuel Moss, *Annals of the United State Christian Commission* (Philadelphia: J. B. Lippincott & Co., 1868), 117.

[13] Mrs. William E. Boardman, *Life and Labors of the Rev. W. E. Boardman* (New York: Appleton and Company, 1887), 99-101; William E. Boardman, *A Higher Christian Life* (New York: D. Appleton, 1859).

and the Army from demoralization." Only salaried staff could guarantee the necessary efficiency. Frederick Law Olmsted, the executive secretary, abruptly turned down the services of his friend, Charles Loring Brace, telling him, "Mercenaries are better than any gratuitous volunteers. I have therefore abandoned volunteers. Don't want them. Consequently...I don't want you...Any man without a clearly defined function about the army is a nuisance, and is treated as such."

The Sanitary Commission studiously avoided maudlin personal appeals. Charles Stillé, the official historian, proudly claimed that "every call for support ever issued under authority of the Commission...rel[ied] mainly on the cold-blooded proposition that every National soldier is a costly piece of National property, worth a certain large number of dollars to the Nation, and that his death is a pecuniary loss." Agent Joseph Parrish wrote approvingly that, "the people want cold, hard figures and realities, not so much stories and sentimentalities."[14]

At first, the Christian Commission differentiated its work from the more established competitor by contrasting its care of men's souls with the USSC provision for soldiers' physical needs. Yet, the distribution of Bibles and tracts scarcely set it apart from the older American Tract and Bible Societies. Faced with a "general confusion" over its mission, the USCC discovered an institutional identity with an embrace of traditional charitable methods that carried an implicit criticism of the Sanitary Commission.

First, the Christian Commission compared its use of volunteers with the Sanitary Commission's large permanent paid staff. Robert Parvin, an Episcopal minister, noted, "It is the distinctive feature of the United States Christian Commission that it sends not its goods by agents who are paid for this purpose, but it sends them by Christian ministers and Christian laymen who volunteer their services to deliver these goods to the men themselves, who are in need of them."

This struck a responsive chord with the general public. Walt Whitman, working as a nurse in Union hospitals, contrasted the two agencies:

---

[14] Brace later served as a USCC delegate. Emma Brace, *Life of Charles Loring Brace* (New York: Charles Scribner's, 1894), 248; Sanitary Commission *Bulletin*, I (1 November 1863), 1; Charles Stillé, *History of the United States Sanitary Commission in the War of the Rebellion* (New York: 1866), 469; Joseph Parrish to Louisa Lee Schuyler, 6 January 1865, Box 669, USSC Papers, New-York Historical Society.

As to the Sanitary Commission & the like, I am sick of them all, & so would not accept any of their berths—you ought to see the way the men as they lie helpless in bed turn their faces from the sight of these Agents...(hirelings as Elias Hicks would call them—they seem to me always a set of foxes & wolves)—they get well-paid...As I told you before the only good fellows I have met are the Christian Commissioners—they go everywhere and receive no pay.

The USSC retorted that slapdash management wasted supplies, claiming, "The system of a voluntary agency is more expensive than that of a compensated agency."[15]

Second, the Sanitary Commission saw their organization as an adjunct of the military quartermaster's office, and dispensed medical supplies, food, and clothing through formal channels, and only after a requisition from appropriate military authorities. They opposed restricted gifts, refusing, for example, to permit local aid societies from the designation of donations directly to hometown military units. The Christian Commission, however, handed gifts directly to the soldiers. Andrew Cross, a Baltimore Commission worker, labeled the Sanitary regulations as "red tapeism which would suffer a patient to starve to death, while the goods rotted on hand, waiting for those requisitions to come."[16]

As they stepped into direct conflict with the more powerful Sanitarians, the Christian Commission raised the ire of the older organization. Henry Bellows fired off a letter to William Dodge, a USCC board member, saying, "I think the Christian Commission, without accomplishing its own object, will weaken and defeat ours." One New York woman warned the national office, "The Christian Commission...is doing the Sanitary much harm...Its members may be well-meaning & conscientious but their attempt to distract the public sympathies and contributions, seems to me not only very unwise but highly mischievous."[17]

[15] Walt Whitman, The Correspondence, ed. Edwin Haviland Miller, 6 vols. (New York: New York University Press, 1961-1977), I, 110-11; J. A. Anderson, "Paid and Unpaid Agents," Sanitary Commission Bulletin, 3 (15 January 1865), 941-43; "The Two Commissions—Comparative Economy," Ibid., 943.

[16] Andrew Cross, The Battle of Gettysburg and the Christian Commission (Baltimore: n.p., 1864), 18.

In private, anger boiled over. Charles Stillé complained,

> It seems true that the very word Christian is used by many as a pretext
> to seduce large numbers of people to pursue most unchristian-like
> conduct…All ideas of fitness, practiced usefulness, efficiency or of
> anything else essential to the success of the object in view are wholly
> ignored, when some vague, musty notion arises in the mind that a
> "Christian" mode of doing it has been suggested which must necessarily
> be the best.[18]

Since the small local aid societies at the heart of the Sanitary Commission
never fully embraced the philosophy of its national leaders, the Christian
Commission appeals drove a subtle wedge between the New York office and
its primary base of support.

Even as they sharpened the "market niche" of the Commission, Stuart and
Boardman overhauled its volunteer program. In the first year of the war,
representatives went to the front with little direction. Volunteers operated
under a "company" plan in which they traveled to military camps and
hospitals in informal groups for an indeterminate length of time. On arrival
at a military camp, the company leader needed to establish a base of operations and secure the necessary passes. Each company or individual decided
the actual day-to-day work schedules, leaving the work wildly uneven in its
execution.

John Adams Cole, a twenty-five-year-old delegate from Massachusetts,
developed a plan to place a paid field agent in each major military department.
In turn, that field agent would designate an unpaid delegate to manage
permanent stations within these units. Faced with uncertain turnover in the
volunteer staff, the Commission requested that delegates commit to a term
no less than six weeks. Cole received an appointment as the first paid field
agent in March 1863 and began immediate implementation of his plan in the
relatively stable winter camps of the Army of the Potomac.[19]

---

[17] Richard Lowitt, *A Merchant Prince of the Nineteenth Century* (New York: Columbia
    University Press, 1945), 220; Emily Barnes to Louisa Lee Schuyler, 16 February 1863,
    Box 674, USSC Papers.

[18] Charles Stillé to Louisa Schuyler, 16 April 1863, Box 640, USSC Papers.

[19] Moss, *Annals of the Christian Commission*, 144-146.

It was a remarkably successful operation. This short-term, six-week mission attracted thousands of volunteers, drawn from ministers and lay leaders, who generally represented the mainstream Baptist, Congregational, Episcopal, Lutheran, Methodist, and Presbyterian denominations. Unitarians, on the other hand, were not welcomed. These delegates played an important intermediary role, bringing news from home to the soldiers—acting as "a living electric chain between the hearth and the tent." When the delegates returned after six weeks, they spoke at local churches, sharing news from the front. These reports provided the civilian population with personal and direct knowledge of the war, often told in the simple anecdotal style of a good minister. Generally educated and well practiced in the pulpit or the Sunday School room, delegates knew how to capture small moments and turn them into heart-rending moral lessons. Unlike Sanitary Commission reports, they readily embraced emotional appeals.[20]

Stuart and Boardman had a canny ear for public opinion and used the press to trumpet the work. The Commission issued a leather bound journal to each delegate in which they recorded their activities at the front. When their terms ended, the central office staff took the diaries, edited selections for publication, and printed copies for distribution to secular and religious newspapers. At the Bank Street headquarters, one corner was devoted to a pigeonholed wooden case, with slots marked for some sixty newspapers.[21]

One issue left unresolved was the role of women. None served on the governing board. Through 1863 the Commission issued official credentials to only twelve women delegates, all but one from the Midwest. The organization reflected its YMCA roots and its audience—men in military camps—and encouraged a culture of masculine piety. For example, one delegate described a typical mid-week church prayer meeting filled with "icy chillness" and attended by "two dozen women and two or three men." In contrast, he wrote, "Soldier's meetings are full of love and glow with earnestness."[22]

Still, the leaders showed little resistance to women's service—only to formal enrollment as delegates. Before the war, William Boardman worked closely with his wife, Mary, and assisted her writing career. Evangelicals strongly

---

[20] USCC, *Second Annual Report*, 13.

[21] James Grant, *The Flag and the Cross*, 18; USCC, *Second Annual Report*, 241.

[22] Alvin Duane Smith, "Two Civil War Notebooks of James Russell Miller," *Journal of the Presbyterian Historical Society* (1959), 72.

supported the Philadelphia Ladies' Aid Society led by Eliza Harris. "Nothing that woman could do was left undone by Mrs. Harris," Lemuel Moss wrote in the Commission's official history, "and much was done by her that few others would have thought of or attempted." The Maryland Committee printed numerous accounts of women's hospital work, including that of Jane C. Moore and her daughter, Jane Boswell Moore. The Chicago Committee bestowed delegate status to several women, including Emma Moody, wife of Dwight Moody.[23]

With its new leadership and organizational structure, the Christian Commission emerged as a significant benevolent institution in the spring of 1863. The battle of Gettysburg proved its most important testing ground and, ultimately, its greatest success.

At Gettysburg

A battle was imminent. That much was clear to the Christian Commission leaders as they read the dispatches reporting the movements of the Army. One delegate wrote, "Everything was now veiled in obscurity; none could tell where the enemy were. Rumors of all sorts filled the air." Workers gathered supplies in warehouses near railroads, not knowing their ultimate destination.[24]

Two delegates from Maine, moving north with the Army of the Potomac, were the first to reach Gettysburg. On leave from his studies at Bangor Theological Seminary, John C. Chamberlain marched to the battle with his brothers in the Twentieth Maine Regiment. After his brother, Colonel Joshua L. Chamberlain, ordered him to the rear, he made his way to the makeshift hospital of the Fifth Corps. "Then came the wounded," he wrote, "they were lying under every tree, the woods seemed full of them, they issued from every path and were scattered along the road-sides."[25]

Rowland Howard, another graduate of Bowdoin and Bangor, arrived on July 1 with the First Corps, commanded by his brother, General Oliver O. Howard. As the battle raged, Howard walked through the streets, stumbling across wounded soldiers. "I attempted," he wrote, "almost alone, the work of relief...I heard in each discharge the possible knell of friend or brother."

---

[23] Mrs. W. E. Boardman, *Life of the Rev. W. E. Boardman*, 96-116; Moss, *Annals*, 74.

[24] USCC, *Second Annual Report*, 44.

[25] John C. Chamberlain to Charles Demond, 11 July 1863, newspaper clipping, Edward Tobey Papers, Massachusetts Historical Society, Boston, MA.

He spent the next two nights at Henry Beitler's home where he offered his service to the doctors. One woman described the scene, writing, "They had a big wagon shed where they brought the wounded and took off their limbs and threw them into the corn crib, and when they had a two horse load, they hauled them away." On the second day of the battle, Howard and Chamberlain met at a field hospital.[26]

As word of the battle filtered back to Washington, Baltimore, and Philadelphia, Commission workers headed for the train depots. In the wake of the invasion, however, no direct railroad lines were open to Gettysburg. A contingent led by Jerome B. Stillson, a delegate from Rochester, New York, took a train north from Baltimore to the town of Westminster, where the line ended.

When they arrived there on July 3, the last day of the battle, they found hundreds of casualties among the chaos. Stillson reported, "There were no surgeons here; we at once entered upon the work of dressing their wounds." General Winfield Scott Hancock, wounded in defense of the Union center, arrived at Westminster at three o'clock in the morning on July 4. Stillson washed clotted blood and dust off the General, and then gave him food and clean clothes. Andrew Cross, a Presbyterian minister from Maryland, arrived on Saturday morning. After waiting all night at the Baltimore train depot, he finally secured a ride. He wrote, "We first entered a burden car, but soon found it would be more comfortable, though a little more dangerous, on the top. Tired of walking all night, and anxious to get on in any way, the top of the car became quite comfortable."[27]

From Westminster, delegates searched for transportation to Gettysburg. I. O. Sloan and Walter Alexander climbed into an ambulance, only to have the horses collapse just outside of town. Leaving the wagon, they walked twenty miles to Gettysburg in a driving rain. Stillson and Griffith Owen also arrived on Saturday afternoon. When Andrew Cross reached Gettysburg, he walked over the battlefield, offering bread and water, later remembering that Sunday as "the first Sabbath we ever recollect spending in bodily labor."[28]

---

[26] Rowland B. Howard, *At Gettysburg* (Boston: American Peace Society, 1887), 2; Elizabeth Thorn, article, *Gettysburg Compiler*, 26 July 1905.

[27] Maryland Committee, *Second Annual Report*, 18-19.

[28] I. O. Sloan, "Letter from Gettysburg," *Lutheran Observer*, 14 August 1863. J. E. Adams stated that Rev. Isaac P. Cook of Baltimore was also at Gettysburg on July 4.

On Monday, Frederic Shearer, the Commission's paid agent in Washington, D. C., arrived in Gettysburg and took over general management of the relief work. Quickly, he established a temporary headquarters in the office of Robert G. Harper, editor of the *Adams Sentinel.* Shearer then negotiated the use of a large storehouse on the central square, owned by Martin Stoever, a professor at Gettysburg College, but rented at that time to merchant John Schick. Before nightfall, fifteen loads of provisions arrived. This was the first relief depot in Gettysburg until the Adams' Express Company opened another warehouse twenty-four hours later.

By Wednesday, July 8, rail lines opened to a point within a mile of town and relief workers and supplies flooded into Gettysburg. Samuel Farrand made his way from New Jersey, climbing aboard a cattle car near York at one A. M. At Hanover Junction, he watched train loads of wounded soldiers pass, going in the opposite direction. "The train," he wrote, "gave me the first realization of the slaughter of the battlefield. It seems that there must be some great reservoir of wounded men." Robert Parvin, rector of St. Paul's Episcopal Church in Cheltenham, Pennsylvania, led some sixty volunteers from Phila-delphia. Climbing off the train, they marched the remaining mile into town. As they approached the city limits, Parvin saw a sign posted by Shearer at the tollgate, directing Christian Commission workers to Schick's Store.[29]

After Parvin's arrival, an informal coordinating committee met to establish a system to handle the influx of men and material, agreeing to leave top-level management to the paid field agents. Shearer, a twenty-five-year-old graduate of the College of New Jersey, took charge of the general operations, assisted by Reverend Edward F. Williams, a paid agent from Massachusetts. They assigned twenty-five-year-old James R. Miller, who held the salaried post of Assistant Field Agent, with coordination of the distribution of supplies. The committee named local resident Robert McCreary as receiving agent, charged with shipping and storage. Although George Stuart arrived in Gettysburg on July 18, he left management to this team, giving his time to hospital visits and a sermon on the Center Square.[30]

[29] Samuel Farrand Diary, Hiram Farrand Papers, Huntington Library, San Marino, CA.

[30] Maryland Committee, *Second Annual Report,* 19; "Our Sick and Wounded—Labors of the Christian Commission," newspaper clipping, Tobey Papers, MHS. This report stated that the committee met in the parlor of "Mr. Cooper's," possibly the home of James Cooper on York Street.

Within days, several hundred ministers, physicians, and lay volunteers arrived in Gettysburg to assist the Commission. Robert Parvin said, "Every train that came in following brought more and still more, while our number of sixty increased to hundreds, men who could be divided up and distributed to the different corps hospitals." In the end, three hundred and fifty-six delegates served in Gettysburg with fifty to sixty women volunteers.[31]

The arriving wagons and trains brought scores of women. Clarissa Jones rushed to the Christian Commission offices after hearing news of the battle. She recalled, "The Christian Commission in Phila[delphia] sent no females to the Battlefields, when I applied to Mr. Geo. H. Stuart for a Pass as Nurse to go to Gettysburg, he directed me to Mr. G. S. Griffith in Baltimore. Mr. Griffith very promptly accepted my services and directly obtained transportation for me." To a later offer of services, Stuart responded that, "the Commission never employs ladies as nurses. Our work is altogether with delegates who are ministers and laymen."[32]

Although no women received official delegate credentials at Gettysburg, dozens served informally with the Commission. Indeed, leaders welcomed their efforts. John Chamberlain commented favorably on the work of Isabella Fogg and Charlotte McKay. George Bringhurst accompanied Emily Souder from Philadelphia to Gettysburg and asked for her assistance in the Fifth Corps Hospital. Jonathan Adams worked with the Moores and obtained Cornelia Hancock's autograph for a list of Christian Commission workers in the Second Corps hospital. Reports widely praised the four Baltimore women who ran a Hanover Junction relief station. One observer noted, "The only hospitals…that were properly managed were those in which ladies were engaged in their attendance upon the sufferers."[33]

The task was daunting. The battle left 14,000 wounded Union soldiers and the retreating Confederates abandoned an additional 6,800 wounded. When Meade ordered the army to pursue the enemy, the medical department went with them, leaving only 106 military surgeons in Gettysburg. As volunteers

---

[31] Ibid.

[32] Eileen F. Conklin, *Women at Gettysburg, 1863* (Gettysburg: Thomas Publications, 1993), 296; George H. Stuart to Miss Mary A. Watson, 1 October 1864, USCC Records, National Archives.

[33] Maryland Committee, *Second Annual Report*, 20, 22, 29.

arrived, the first reaction was one of horror at the carnage. John Foster described a scene in the Second Corps hospital:

> The rebel surgeons piled the ground-floor with their wounded, placing them so thickly that it was almost impossible for one to stir without communicating a shock to all. In the centre of the floor, the surgeons planted a table for amputating purposes; and there, in full view of hundreds of enfeebled wretches, the process of cutting, and carving, and butchering (for it was nothing else) went on day after day. The scene was…horrible. It was torture for the faint, disheartened wounded to lie, hour after hour, perfectly helpless, compulsory witnesses of the atrocities which these surgeons dignified by the name of operations. During every minute of fifteen hours every day some sufferer was upon the table. Groans, shrieks, and curses constantly filled the air, the sound of the knife and crash of the saw blending continuously with the din of agony. Legs and arms falling from the table to the floor beneath were raked out in armfuls, with every eye fixed on the spectacle, and carried away for burial.[34]

Emily Souder covered her ears with a pillow at night, hoping to block out the cries from a nearby hospital. She wrote, "But who shall describe the horrible atmosphere which meets us almost continually? Chloride of lime has been freely used in the broad streets of the town and to-day the hospital was much improved by the same means; but it is needful to close the eyes on sights of horror and to shut the ears against sounds of anguish and to extinguish, as far as possible, the sense of smelling."[35]

In the first three weeks, the Army organized its medical care by corps, with field hospitals attached to each unit. Hundreds of small makeshift hospitals dotted the town as soldiers carried the wounded into the nearest building—the College, Seminary, Court House, Public School, Lutheran, Catholic and Presbyterian Churches, hotels, warehouses, private homes, depots, barns, stables, and tents.[36]

[34] John Y. Foster, "Four Days at Gettysburg," *Harper's Weekly*, February 1864.

[35] Emily Souder, *Leaves from the Battlefield of Gettysburg. A Series of Letters from a Field Hospital and National Poems* (Philadelphia: C. Sherman, Son & Co., 1864), 23.

[36] Cross, *Battle of Gettysburg*, 17; See Gregory A. Coco, *A Vast Sea of Misery* (Gettysburg: Thomas Publications, 1988)

The Commission established stations in each corps hospital (except for the Sixth Corps) under the supervision of an experienced delegate. The committee split the volunteers into companies of five to six people, appointed a captain for the unit, and then assigned work sites. Some delegates slept in nearby homes, others in hospital tents.[37]

Two warehouses, located in the center of town, were hubs of activity. Shearer posted daily work schedules on the front door. Inside,

> The storehouses of the Commission in Gettysburg presented the busiest of all the busy scenes in the town. They had been perhaps the largest sale establishments in Gettysburg. The shelves were well supplied with soft bread, which was craved by all the inmates of the hospitals, and with every variety of hospital stores. The delegates of the Commission, or persons bearing their orders, disabled soldiers, who were able to walk, and visitors in search of their relatives and friends among the wounded, were passing rapidly in and out of the premises all the day through, and during the earlier hours of the night.

The managers directed every hospital to send a delegate to the warehouses each morning with a list of needed goods. Andrew Cross wrote, "It was often amusing to see the delegates that came in from each of these hospitals daily to receive such supplies as were needed. A mother could not have been more anxious for the supply to her children than these men were to procure whatever would make comfortable the wounded in their particular district."[38]

McCreary secured a site next to the Gettysburg depot of the Hanover Railroad to receive incoming shipments. This became an unexpected gathering place, as soldiers left the hospitals and milled around for hours, waiting for a train out of town. Louis Muller, a Maryland delegate, set up an "eating saloon" to feed the troops. He reported, "We have fed at least two thousand wounded men in this town to-day, and about the same number of rations have been sent by our delegates to those in the field. No man can estimate the amount of suffering we are relieving." The USCC eventually turned this operation over to the Sanitary Commission.[39]

---

[37] USCC, *Second Annual Report*, 31; M. Newkirk Jr. to William Boardman, 22 July 1863, USCC Records, National Archives.

[38] Maryland Committee, *Second Annual Report*, 23; Cross, *Battle of Gettysburg*, 18.

In the First Corps, hospitals spread over various sites in the town, including the Catholic Church, the Courthouse, and the Presbyterian Church. Henry Stevens of Blue Hill, Maine, directed the work in the Second Division with help from Alexander McAuley, pastor of the Fifth Reformed Church in Philadelphia. The Commission passed over the Corps' First Division, leaving the work to Elmina Spencer, a New York nurse who regularly traveled with the troops and drew on Commission supplies.

The Second Corps saw the brunt of the action, leaving more than three thousand patients. Thirty years after the battle, Bushrod James, a physician and Commission volunteer from Philadelphia, recalled the scene, writing,

> No written nor expressed language could ever picture the field of Gettysburg! Blood! blood! and tattered flesh! shattered bones and mangled forms almost without the semblance of human beings! faces torn and bruised and lacerated…groans and cries, screams and curses, moans and grinding teeth! And the horrible silence of torture beyond all expression…those sickening weeks of work, when the cut of the knife and the rasp of the saw…grated on my overtaxed nerves.

George Delamater, Chaplain of the Eighth New York Regiment, wrote: "No pen…can describe it. The noble sufferers lay on the ground without shelter. Many destitute of blankets, and some nearly naked. What clothes they had…were saturated with blood and alive with maggots. Incessant rains had saturated the ground on which they lay."[40]

The Commission set up two tents in the First and Second Divisions, under Robert Matlack, an Episcopal minister from Philadelphia, and James Eldredge. Several women worked at this site, including Jane C. Moore, her daughter, Jane Boswell Moore, and Emily Souder. Jonathan Adams and J. B. Stillson pitched a tent in the Third Division, Second Corps, staffed with some dozen delegates. Adams wrote, "We fed the hungry, gave drink to the thirsty, bound up the wounds of the wounded, changed the position of the suffering, and breathed consolation to the disheartened and dying."[41]

[39] Moss, *Annals*, 384; Maryland Committee, *Second Annual Report*, 19.

[40] Bushrod W. James, *Echoes of Battle* (Philadelphia: Henry T. Coates, 1895), 100-101; Maryland Committee, *Second Annual Report*, 87.

[41] USCC, *Second Annual Report*, 251-252; Maryland Comm., *Second Annual Report*, 87.

Disaster struck the Third Corps hospital with its twenty-five hundred wounded. No sooner had Walter Alexander established the station than a drunken officer wandered through the camp and shot him seven times. When delegate Samuel Farrand entered the Corps Hospital on July 10, he found no one in charge, "so went to work each on his own responsibility. Others came and did the same." These new workers filled the gap, so that by July 22, a report stated, "...our work is now going on very harmoniously and the surgeon (Dr. Jewett) expresses himself highly satisfied with the work."[42]

One barn held wounded Confederates, "necessarily neglected by our own over-occupied surgeons." The Commission took over the work:

> Delegates who were physicians were sent to them, who sleeping among them as they could, and eating what was easiest obtained, bound up wounds, amputated limbs, and gave them nourishing soups and stimulating drinks, while they never forgot the religious wants of their patients.[43]

Robert Parvin directed the Fifth Corps hospital work, with some eight hundred patients, succeeded by another Philadelphia minister, Reverend George Bringhurst. The Commission assigned the Sixth Corps to Parvin as well, as it held only a few hundred wounded soldiers.

James Grant of Philadelphia, a former YMCA board member, managed the station in the Eleventh Corps Hospital, which held some eighteen hundred patients. Rev. J. B. Poerner, who worked with Grant, found the men lying in a soggy field, "literally covered in mud and rotten hay or straw, from three to five inches deep." With a squad of volunteers, he rounded up empty boxes, barrels, and fallen timber, and built beds for the wounded. Poerner recorded, "We held daily Divine services, at different places, in the streets of our camp, as to enable every man within the tents to listen to the singing of hymns, prayers, and preaching of God's Word." After four weeks, Poerner collapsed after suffering a bout of typhoid fever.[44]

---

[42] USCC, *Second Annual Report*, 74; Samuel Farrand Diary, Huntington Library; M. Newkirk Jr. to Wm. Boardman, 22 July 1863, USCC Records, National Archives.

[43] USCC, *Second Annual Report*, 75.

[44] USCC, *Second Annual Report*, 72-73; United States Christian Commission for the Army and Navy, *Third Annual Report for the Year 1864* (Philadelphia: USCC, 1865), 265-266.

The Twelfth Corps Hospital, holding some twelve hundred soldiers, drew few supplies or men from the Commission. The reason is unclear, although the Surgeon-in-charge Dr. Goodman complained to the Commission about its "sanitary"–or supply–work. This Corps retained its medical wagons before the battle and probably needed less assistance.[45]

The relief work extended well beyond Gettysburg. At Hanover Junction, along the single rail line from Gettysburg, several Maryland women, directed by Mrs. Alph Hyatt, set up a station to care for the wounded as they passed through to distant permanent military hospitals. Emily Souder, on her way to Gettysburg, described their work:

> A car is stationed here, close to the railroad track, where four ladies from Baltimore prepare lemonade, bread and butter, to refresh the men, besides pies, farina, etc.–"The Christian Commission Car." They have three stations on the way. We made a visit to this car and saw the ladies at work.[46]

In Harrisburg, the Commission set up a "Union Tabernacle" at Camp Curtin. George Stuart reported,

> [The station] has been abundantly manned and supplied; and has served as a shelter for 500 soldiers in a single night; as a place of supply for thousands, a base of operations for delegates going to the front, a voluntary refreshment saloon and resting place for the hungry, thirsty and weary, a place for writing letters home, (stationery furnished gratis) and a church by the way, where thousands daily have heard the gospel and received the Scripture, religious papers, and tracts.[47]

At Carlisle, the rivalry with the Sanitary Commission reared its head. On July 7, Isaac Harris, an agent for the rival organization, wrote in his diary,

---

[45] M. Newkirk, Jr. to William Boardman, 22 July 1863, USCC Records, National Archives.

[46] USCC, *Second Annual Report*, 102; Emily Souder, *Leaves from the Battlefield*, 11-12.

[47] George Stuart to Edward Tobey, 8 July 1863, Tobey Papers, MHS; Army Committee of Western Pennsylvania, *Report of the Army Committee of the U. S. Christian Commission*, Pittsburgh, PA (Pittsburgh: 1863), 8.

The [Christian Commission] were in high spirits when they ascertained that the San. Com. had no stores at Carlisle and hoped by their numbers to supply the Hospital there before I could. The train came to a stand about one mile N. of the town on account of a broken bridge…I left the train and walked into town through a drenching rain to the Hospital. Had a talk with Dr. Tomlinson the Surgeon in charge…Loaded the wagons and drove to the Hospital and was unloading when the CC's again appeared and offered assistance which was refused by Dr. Palmer, saying, the San. Com. had supplied every want of his patients.[48]

In other towns, delegates assisted at small emergency hospitals.

George Stuart led a fund-raising drive, addressing audiences throughout the east. In Pittsburgh, a public meeting resulted in donations of $22,000. On July 6, the Chairman sent a telegraph to Boston, declaring,

Our victory is complete and glorious. Our loss is fearful. The enemies wounded in our hands. We have about one hundred delegates on the battlefield and a hundred more offering. Raise and send us from Boston ten thousand dollars. Our own people are doing nobly. One church not rich gave yesterday a thousand dollars. The want is great.

Within days, the Boston Committee collected $30,000.[49]

In large cities and small towns, the Commission asked churches to gather and pack supplies. At the Ascension Church in Philadelphia, worshipers gathered on Sunday, July 5, waiting to hear news. In place of a sermon, wrote John Foster, "the clergyman had brought a sewing machine; instead of Sabbath-day finery, each woman wore the more royal ornament of plain working apparel. In every available niche a sewing machine was enshrined; even the pulpit desk was removed." Within a week, Foster volunteered to work in the hospitals at Gettysburg.[50]

In Baltimore, Goldsborough Griffith secured the use of Apollo Hall as a supply warehouse, and then placed volunteers at work on the shipping

[48] Isaac Harris, Diary, Harrisburg Public Library, Harrisburg, Pennsylvania.

[49] George Stuart to Edward Tobey and Charles Demond, 6 July 1863, Tobey Papers, MHS; Newspaper clipping, 10 July 1863, Tobey Papers, MHS.

[50] John Y. Foster, "Four Days at Gettysburg," Harper's Weekly, February 1864.

docks. "Every visitor was drafted for service," a report stated. "It was a rare sight presented in the mixed corps of laborers, consisting of ladies, clergymen, teachers, lawyers, merchants, mechanics and colored laborers."[51]

OVER THE FOLLOWING WEEKS, Christian Commission workers labored in the field hospitals. In the face of suffering, their immediate concerns were the physical and medical needs of the wounded. Although not trained in medicine, surgeons enlisted their aid. From the Second Corps hospital, Joseph H. Bradley reported, "…we have also done much here in dressing some of the less complicated wounds. We found very many, especially among the rebels, who had received absolutely no surgical care since they were wounded, which in most cases was from five to six days ago."[52]

Enoch Miller, a private in the 108th New York Volunteer Infantry, lay under a tree with a bullet through his lung. He recalled,

> The Surgeon of our regiment made an examination of my wound, but as I supposed that at that time the ball was in me, he only looked at my breast. He gave me a sleeping powder, and throwing his rubber blanket over me, left me as he supposed, to die. During the next three or four days, without a pillow or sufficient covering, my clothes saturated with my own blood, with no proper food, attended by a faithful comrade, Sergeant John O'Connell, I lay scarcely daring to hope for life.
>
> About noon one day I saw in the distance the silver badge of the Christian Commission, and sending my comrade, I soon had its Delegate by my side. In that Delegate I recognized Brother Stillson. He was an old friend, and we had been co-laborers in the Sunday school work before the war commenced. He knew me in an instant, and without waiting to waste words, supplied me with a feather pillow,—the first I had had in a year,—a quilt, a draught of wine, some nice soft crackers and a cup of warm tea. After offering up an earnest prayer by my side, he hastened away to secure some clean clothes. He then removed my filthy garments, and in doing that, it was found that the ball had passed through me.
>
> After all this had been done, I felt as though I was at home; for, my dear sir, the Delegate of the Commission acts the part of a tender, loving

---

[51] Maryland Committee, *Second Annual Report*, 37.

[52] Joseph H. Bradley to Edward Tobey, 7 July 1863, Tobey Papers, MHS.

mother, a willing father, an affectionate sister, a sympathizing brother and a beloved pastor.[53]

Small, simple good deeds made lasting impressions. Azor Howett Nickerson remembered the potatoes.

I had conceived the idea that there was nothing in the world I wanted or could eat except a roasted potato: and as it was said that there was not a potato to be had within miles of our camp, of course I wanted one more than ever. I had long since ceased asking for them, but when food was mentioned that simple vegetable was the only thing that suggested itself to my mind. My clergyman friend was located in the Second Division hospital, some distance from ours, which was the Third Division, Second Corps. But he always came to see me at least once a day, and I had my tent flaps turned back so that I could watch for his coming. One very hot Sunday morning I caught sight of him coming considerably earlier than was his usual custom. His coat was thrown across his arm, and the perspiration was rolling down his face, but when he looked up and saw me watching his approach he swung a little bundle he had tied in his handkerchief, and exclaimed, with all the enthusiasm of a boy: "I've got them, captain, I've got them!" Sure enough, he soon laid before me a dozen potatoes, two of which he immediately washed with his own hands, and roasted in the ashes. I saw Tiffany's collection of diamonds, at the Centennial of 1876, and also the most notable display of jewels ever made by one person in this country…and yet I have never seen any diamonds, rubies, sapphires, or pearls that were at all comparable with the exquisite beauty of that cluster of Irish potatoes, brought to me at Gettysburg, on Sunday morning, by the Rev. J. E. Adams of New Sharon, Me. He had walked in the broiling sun over ten miles to gratify an invalid's whim.[54]

This simple act validated the Christian Commission's balance of spiritual and temporal care. Nickerson wrote,

[53] Edward P. Smith, *Incidents of the United States Christian Commission* (Philadelphia: J. B. Lippincott & Co., 1869), 160-161. Miller recovered, returned to seminary, and became a chaplain with the 25th U. S. Colored Troops.

[54] Azor Nickerson, "Two Visits to Gettysburg," *Scribner's Magazine*, July 1893, 23-24.

Up to this time he had never held any religious services in my tent. So, while he was preparing another potato for one of my fellow-soldiers, I told the attendant that he might give my compliments to him and say that, as it was Sunday morning, I should be very glad, if he could spare the time, to have him offer a prayer. "Certainly," he replied, when they told him, and walking over to my tent he laid aside his hat and knelt by my rude bunk. He was still without his coat, his sleeves were rolled up, and his hands were grimy with the ashes from his potato roast. His throat was bare of necktie, the collar thrown open wide, and great beads of perspiration stood on his broad forehead; but what a prayer! Like his works it was fervid, earnest, and apropos. Nothing seemed to be forgotten, and yet it appeared to be such a short prayer...When it was finished and the worthy man had gone, I felt as though I had really been with one who walked arm in arm with the Master, and knew when and how to work as well as when and how to pray.

The "comfort-bags" distributed by the Commission perfectly illustrate the desired combination of physical and spiritual care. These small cloth kits usually included thread, sewing needles, small scissors, and scraps of material. Throughout the North, the Christian Commission encouraged Sunday School students to make a "comfort-bag" to send to the Army, then enclose a letter for the recipient. At Gettysburg, a wounded Confederate received a comfort-bag from a little girl in Massachusetts. He wrote to her:

My Dear Little Friend:—I received your present, the comfort-bag, and it is thrice welcome, although it was intended for Union defenders. It was given to me by a Christian woman, who lost her holy anger against Rebels—for such am I—in her bounteous sympathy with the unfortunate. My little friend can imagine my thankfulness for the favor, when I inform her that I have no friends this side of heaven—all gone, father, mother, sister and brother, and I am all alone.

The dear comfort-bag I shall always keep as a memento of true sympathy from a generous heart in the loyal State of Massachusetts. I hope you will not be disappointed by this, coming as it does from a Rebel; for I was forced into the ranks at the point of the bayonet, for I would not go willingly to fight against the dear old flag, whose ample folds have always shielded the orphan and made glad the oppressed.

I have read your note very many times over, and have wished it could rightfully be mine. "Do they think of me at home?" Silence—all is silence! Not so with the Union soldier; a thousand tokens tell him yes.

I was wounded in the second day's fight, and am now packing up my all to be exchanged or sent back a cripple for life. I am seventeen years old, and now am turned out with one arm to carve my way through the world; but my trust is in my heavenly Father, who will forgive and bless. Hoping that God may in mercy reunite us all again as brothers and sisters, I am your unworthy friend,

E – A – Co. –, Miss. Volunteers[55]

Although they cared for temporal needs, men's souls were the Commission's central work. "There is no more dangerous duty allotted to any man to perform," wrote J. R. Miller, "than the duty of directing dying men to Christ. It is dangerous because of the terrible consequences of a mistake."[56]

George Stuart came to Gettysburg for several days in the middle of July. After speaking to a crowd in the central square, he visited the hospitals. As he passed one patient, the man called out, "Ain't you going to stop and talk to me?" Stuart stopped and turned to him. The man, William Doubleday, told Stuart that he had never made a profession of faith, but added that he was not a "wicked man." Doubleday confessed that his wife prayed for his salvation, both physical and spiritual. Stuart related the soldier's story:

> "When I enlisted," said he, "which I did because I considered it a disgrace to be drafted, just as I was leaving for the war, my wife said, 'I hope you will come back all right, and a good Christian.' It touched my heart. We went into the room with the family, and there, she prayed for me, and then asked me to pray. I tried to offer a few broken petitions. My little boy, only thirteen years old, then offered a most earnest prayer for me and for our distressed country. I don't know where he learned to pray like that, unless it was in the Sabbath-school."
>
> When he learned how I was connected with the Commission, and saw the badge, tears came to his eyes. When I spoke to him of Jesus, he pressed

---

[55] Smith, *Incidents* (Philadelphia: J. B. Lippincott & Co., 1869), 178.

[56] James Russell Miller, Notebooks, Presbyterian Historical Society.

[57] Edward P. Smith, *Incidents*, 170-171.

my hands, and the tears came fast as rain. I prayed with him, and then he asked me to bend down and kiss him. He died soon after from the effects of an amputation. I received a letter from his wife, who came to him before his death. She was very earnest in her expressions of thankfulness, and told me with loving sorrow and joy how her husband's peaceful death had answered her prayers.[57]

Reverend Martin Stoever—Lutheran scholar and professor at Gettysburg College—found that traditional ecclesiastical boundaries disappeared in the face of death. On Sunday, July 5, he attended to the soldiers in a hospital located in the St. Francis Xavier Catholic Church. He recalled,

> On entering the building, filled with wounded and dying, I was met by a Roman Catholic lady, well known to me as a good woman, but a very rigid religionist. She said at once, "Do come and speak to this man. The Surgeon says he will die, and he is unconverted." I followed her to the chancel within which he was lying. She introduced me as a Protestant, connected with the college, and then left him to my attention. I presented to him the only way opened for his return to God, and kneeling by his side, prayed with him, the first prayer doubtless ever offered by a Protestant in that church, and that at the request of one of its members. The man died shortly afterwards most peacefully, trusting in Christ and with the hope of eternal life.[58]

Thoughts often turned to home. Delegates sat with the wounded, writing letters to mothers and fathers, sisters and brothers, wives and lovers. On his deathbed, Oliver Stephens told Jonathan Adams, "I want you to write my mother that I die for my country…I am perfectly happy." Andrew Cross sent five hundred letters to the Baltimore post office within the first days of his service. Clarissa Jones wrote nearly one hundred letters "to relieve the anxiety, and alas,…to announce 'the saddest ends of all the fears' of mothers, wives, daughters and sisters far away."[59]

[58] Ibid., 168-169.

[59] Jonathan E. Adams Diary, Special Collections, Bowdoin College, Brunswick, Maine; Cross, *Battle of Gettysburg*, 23; Jane Boswell Moore, "Our Country," *Lutheran Observer*, 25 September 1863.

Delegates often addressed a common concern—whether the soldier had performed honorably and manfully during the battle. Robert Parvin found David Laird, a Michigan soldier, on the battlefield. As Laird lay in a hospital, Parvin visited him regularly. The minister wrote, "At first he was very much troubled because his wound—a serious one received while the regiment was falling back under orders—was in the back. I reassured him, and explained all the circumstances to his parents in thy letter."

His parents responded with assurances. His father wrote, "As to David's wound in his back, it need give him no uneasiness. None who know him will suppose it to be there on account of cowardice." His mother wrote, "My dear one, you have done what you could to suppress this cruel rebellion. May God comfort you! You are still serving the country so dear to your heart. You have been for thirty months an active volunteer; now you are a suffering one." His parents traveled to the front and arrived to see their son die.[60]

To dying believers, the delegates spoke words of consolation and companionship. William Eva, a Presbyterian minister from Kensington, Pennsylvania, recalled a visit with two men at Gettysburg:

> Away in the corner of a shed crowded with wounded, I found a dying man. His limbs were already cold and the death-damp was upon his brow. Fellow-sufferers were thick enough about him, yet he was dying alone. He was still conscious when I came to him,—not only conscious, but happy in the love of God. I can truly say that nowhere have I witnessed a more triumphant peace than his. We prayed by his side, and then sang!
>
> "Just as I am, without one plea,"
>
> with the chorus
>
> "Happy day! happy day! When Jesus washed my sins away."
>
> As we prayed and sang, the Holy Spirit seemed to come down not only upon the dying man, but on all in that dolorous place; and here and there, from among the wounded braves as they lay upon the floor, was uttered aloud the earnest cry, "God have mercy on my soul!"[61]

As word spread throughout the north, families journeyed to Gettysburg to find brothers, sons and husbands, often seeking out a Christian Commission

---

[60] Ibid., 166.

[61] Ibid., 172-172.

badge. Many times, delegates gave families the first news of the death of a loved one. On one page of his diary, Jonathan Adams listed:

> Mr. Gant came for his son. N. J. Mr. Fasset came for his son. Pen. Mrs. Scott came for her husband from Maine. Miss Allen came for her bro. Mich. All dead. Mr. Downs came for his son. Saw him alive. Carried him away dead.[62]

On the day that Captain Charles Billings of Chamberlain's Twentieth Maine Regiment died, Robert Parvin heard a knock at ten o'clock as he sat writing letters. He opened the door to find the dead man's brother, who had accompanied the Captain's wife to Gettysburg. He told Parvin, "I have buoyed her up this long way with the hope that we would find the Captain in good condition. Where is he, sir?" Parvin gave him the tragic news. "Oh!" said the man, "I cannot tell her! I cannot tell her! I cannot trust myself to tell her, or even to see her again, to-night!" He begged the minister to return with him to break the news to the widow, which Parvin did.[63]

Andrew Cross remembered one woman who came to nurse her husband, only to learn that he was dead. She asked to be taken to his grave, but was told that it was impossible to find him, remarking, "You might as well expect to find a needle in a hay-stack."

> "Is it as likely?" she said. He said, "just as likely." "Then," said she, "I can find him, for I could take apart every blade of hay until I had removed it entirely. Show me where he was buried?" She got help to go with her, and after disinterring some 12 to 22, as they had nearly uncovered the next body, she espied something by which she knew him, and jumping down into the grave, with her own hand scratched off the earth that covered his arm and aided in getting him out, and thus bore home with her the object of affection.[64]

Delegates conducted many graveside services. In the Fifth Corps, George Bringhurst presided over the funeral of a young soldier from Maine, "whom we had tenderly nursed, and learned to love. Many an eye, unused to weeping,

[62] Jonathan E. Adams Diary, Special Collections, Bowdoin College.

[63] Smith, *Incidents*, 171-172. Billings died on 15 July 1863.

[64] Cross, *Battle of Gettysburg*, 26.

was glazed, at that solemn twilight hour, as over his silent form our voices blended in singing those touching words, 'There is rest for the weary.'"[65]

Clarissa Jones told the story of a young Virginian who, after watching his brother fall in the battle, surrendered to the Federal soldiers so that he could be with him. When the rebel soldier died four days later, a few workers gathered at his grave. She wrote:

> Major Holstein and his wife read the burial service each day over the long stretch of dead, and Mrs. Moore and I always accompanied them. But at this particular time, Major Holstein did not have his glasses with him, and could not read without them. They were preparing to bury the boy without any service. As soon as the brother realized this, he sat on a log and cried as though his heart would break. Finally he regained his composure and, looking up, said, "Is there not somebody who will say a word over my brother?"…Miss Moore and I could not resist this appeal. Major Holstein let us have his book, and we read the burial service.[66]

It took an emotional toll on the workers. When the brother told Jones that he intended to escape and return home, she recalled, "We said nothing. We let him go. No one told on the poor fellow." One afternoon, Jonathan Adams came across the graves of two Maine men that he knew. "Was overcome for the moment," he wrote, "Tuesday morn went out & sodded the grave of Smith & McCobb."[67]

Commission workers questioned the meaning of their work, asking where God's hand was in the midst of all the suffering. Andrew Cross pondered the moral implications of the war. "This war was to accomplish God's purpose," he argued. "We had gotten rich, proud and corrupt;…the young had taken control of their parents, defying law and order, and making rebellion against God and the laws of the nation honorable." Not everyone shared this view. Bushrod James met an "eminently pious lady" who stated that she "never could reconcile the idea in her mind of a Christian going into the army to fight" and doubted "the piety of all fighting men." Rowland Howard, horrified by the violence, became Secretary of the American Peace Society after the

[65] Rev. George Bringhurst to George Stuart, 3 August 1863, Tobey Papers, MHS.

[66] Clarissa Fellows Jones, Pension file, submitted 5 February 1917, National Archives.

[67] Jonathan E. Adams Diary, Special Collections, Bowdoin College.

war. He wrote, "[War] lacks not only kindness and humanity; it lacks mercy, righteousness, justice—it is a moral monster. However justifiable we think its alleged cause, its facts are hideously wicked."[68]

The greatest controversy concerned the care of the wounded Confederate soldiers. If the war was part of God's plan, and God favored the Union, then how should a Christian treat the enemy? The arguments were not theoretical, since many southerners would return to their units and aim their rifles at Union soldiers again. Clarissa Jones wrote,

> The Union men could not understand my devotion to the Confederates, and finally I noticed among them a coldness to me. I asked them what was the trouble, and one of them said, 'Miss Jones, where are you from?' I told them I was from Philadelphia. 'Are you a rebel sympathizer?' another asked. I answered most decidedly, no. And then I had a heart to heart talk with them, and told them of the sufferings of the rebels and how desperately they needed the affectionate care of a woman.[69]

The anger was palpable in a letter that Hospital Steward Charles Merrick of the Eighth Ohio sent home to his wife. Describing the Third Division, Second Corps Hospital, he wrote,

> Our boys are very indignant at the conduct of the "Christian Sanitary Commissions." They devote almost their whole time to the rebels—give them everything to eat and wear—preach and pray with them—but pay very little attention to our men. I have watched them close and bear testimony against them. Not once have they had singing and praying among the Union boys. Is it not a compliment to us? Are we so good we do not need their missionary labors? I don't complain on this point, but I do complain that our boys have not had their share of the comforts, the delicacies, the attention they bestow on the rebels...These are facts. They will doctor up the rebels and send them back into their ranks to shoot us down with less mercy than ever.[70]

[68] Bushrod James, *Echoes of Battle*, 133; Rowland Howard, "At Gettysburg," 3.

[69] *Philadelphia North American*, 29 June 1913, special section, 4.

[70] Charles H. Merrick to Dr. Myra H. Merrick, 12 July 1863, William P. Palmer Collection, Western Reserve Historical Society, Cleveland, Ohio.

To deter criticism, the delegates related stories of the redeeming power of their work. One wrote, "Tears coursed down their cheeks, and the 'God bless you' often fell from their lips, and in some instances they added, 'God bless your cause.' Your Commission is bringing these rebels to a better mind…they never can forget the Spirit of the Master evinced by the Commission."[71]

The Christian approach, the Commission argued, tempered the rebels' hard-hearted views. One delegate told of an encounter with an South Carolina officer, who, after refusing offers of assistance, finally broke down, and said, amidst his tears, "I can't understand you Yankees; you fight us like devils, and then you treat us like angels. I am sorry I entered this war."[72]

As VOLUNTEERS streamed into Gettysburg, the field agents could not properly evaluate prospective delegates. The best were "not afraid of blood, work, or sin," as one observer wrote. However, many entered the ranks who were unsuited to the work. Shearer complained to George Stuart that,

> Today there came into the office a man badly intoxicated, though able to attend to business, representing that the Provost Marshal would not furnish him without artifact from my self, affirming that he was connected with us. His words were so full of awful and repeated oaths that I was compelled to say that his conduct would induce me to recall any commission that he might have.[73]

He reported that some twenty men were "distasteful to the military authorities, who had been in our midst as delegates of the Baltimore Committee." He came across three young men at Hanover Junction, apparently with delegate credentials, who appeared "exceedingly wicked." Goldsborough Griffith confronted a Reverend Smith, a delegate from New Jersey, about some slanderous gossip directed at another delegate. Later, when Griffith found Smith in an inebriated stupor, he sent him home.[74]

---

[71] Tobey Papers, MHS.

[72] Edward P. Smith, *Incidents*, 177.

[73] Beriah B. Hotchkin to William Boardman, 22 July 1863, USCC Records, National Archives; Frederic E. Shearer to George H. Stuart, 20 July 1862, USCC Records, National Archives.

[74] Ibid.; G. S. Griffith to George H. Stuart, 1 September 1863, USCC Records, NA.

Some volunteers were shirkers. The chief agent at Hagerstown, Beriah Hotchkin, found one delegate,

> …sitting in our only chair, from three to five hours a day—the rest of the time, much to our relief, invisible…on Monday I got him to accompany a soldier's corpse to the grave, despairing of getting any other service from him. On Tuesday we had another funeral. I asked him to go. "No!" said he. "I believe not. I walked there yesterday a mile in the hot sun, and I believe I shant do it today."[75]

Others proved sanctimonious with few interpersonal skills, alienating the soldiers with pious words without supporting works. Azor Howett Nickerson complained of one delegate:

> He carried with him a large bible and a hymn-book. I do not recall that he ever brought anything else, or even asked a patient to take a glass of water. When he came in he asked me how I felt, and if I was prepared to die. Then he adjusted his spectacles and read a chapter from his bible. That finished, he selected what seemed to be the longest hymn he could find, and in a wheezy voice sang it all through without skipping a stanza. These interesting exercises were then closed by a lengthy prayer in which advice to the Creator was the most prominent feature. He daily inflicted this programme upon me at a time when every breath I drew was like the thrust of a dozen daggers, until the surgeons finally found it out, and then they forbade his entering my tent at all.[76]

Some enthusiastic delegates, eager to fill all requests, chafed at the strictness of military and medical order and bypassed procedures, drawing the wrath of the doctors. Samuel Farrand noted, "Some delegates of the Commission were quite injudicious in their movements. Stimulants and food were frequently given by them without the knowledge of the surgeons. This might have been avoided by stricter arrangements and method and discipline on the part of the Commission."[77]

[75] B. B. Hotchkin to W. E. Boardman, 22 July 1863, USCC Records, National Archives.

[76] Azor Nickerson, "Personal Recollections of Two Visits to Gettysburg," 24-25.

[77] Samuel Farrand Diary, Huntington Library, San Marino, California

The greatest threat, though, came from southern sympathizers who used the Commission's reputation for compassion to visit the wounded rebels. The Provost-Marshall seized a wagon marked USCC and discovered that it was used to carry forbidden goods to Confederate soldiers. At least one woman, under the guise of the Commission, assisted a southern officer in an escape attempt. In the end, the provost marshal required all workers to take an oath of allegiance. The Commission dismissed anyone who refused.[78]

These reports spread through the army, creating a sense of distrust. The Moores came under suspicion after reports that military authorities arrested a Baltimore woman of that name as a spy. Two months later, Goldsborough Griffith apologized to Stuart for lapses by the Baltimore branch and promised to correct the problem.[79]

Camp Letterman

By late July the Army had transported 16,125 wounded soldiers to the permanent hospitals near Washington, Philadelphia, and Baltimore, leaving nearly four thousand difficult cases. On July 20, the Medical Corps merged the various corps hospitals to one site, known as Camp Letterman. A second hospital remained open in the Lutheran Seminary.

Within days of the move to Camp Letterman, the Commission emptied its supplies from Schick's Store and consolidated operations in a single warehouse. With fewer patients, several delegates, including Shearer and Miller, left town and returned to the Army of the Potomac. On August 7, 1863, the special Gettysburg committee dissolved and turned the work over to a local branch chapter that included Robert McCreary, Martin Stoever, and merchants James Fahnstock and John Schick.[80]

At Camp Letterman, workers established a Christian Commission station, under the supervision of Mattias Willing, a New York minister, with five tents, including sleeping, storage, and eating tents. In the new well-designed camp, the atmosphere of crisis ebbed. For the wounded, death threatened less, replaced by a struggle to accept the prospects of a life as a disabled person. Days became tedious, filled by the Christian Commission with

---

[78] USCC, *Second Annual Report*, 77-8.

[79] G. S. Griffith to George Stuart, 18 September 1863, USCC Records, NA.

[80] M. Newkirk, Jr. to William E. Boardman, 22 July 1863, USCC Records, NA. This second warehouse is described as "on the opposite corner" from Schick's store.

books, newspapers, and pamphlets for the soldiers. Delegates and women volunteers made rounds, often stopping to write letters for the patients.

With little else to do, the soldiers flocked to worship services and prayer meetings. George Bringhurst wrote,

> I preached in eight tents, while other delegates of the Commission were engaged in a similar manner. In the evening a prayer meeting convened …Prayers were offered, and the congregation, consisting of several hundred soldiers and citizens, united in singing some sweet hymns. We continued our meeting until the stars came out and seemed to join in the Doxology. When we closed, the soldiers pled with us to have such services frequently.[81]

At the Seminary Hospital, I. O. Sloan supervised the work, directing eight delegates and six to eight women volunteers. Of the one hundred patients, half were Confederates. One Commission delegate found an unusually receptive audience among the enemy. Rev. George Junkin was the father-in-law of General Thomas "Stonewall" Jackson and had staunchly opposed secession while President of Washington College in Lexington, Virginia.

As August gave way to September, the number of patients dropped daily. Those remaining fell into doldrums and depression after almost three months in confinement. To lighten the dark mood of the hospital, the Commission sponsored a grand celebration at Camp Letterman on September 23. Anna Holstein noted,

> The day selected, proving bright and balmy, tempted many, who had not yet ventured outside their tents, into the open air, hoping they might be able to participate in the promised enjoyments. The streets and tents of the hospital had been decorated with evergreens, and everything on this gala day had a corresponding cheerful look. Hospital life, with its strict military rule, is so wearisome and monotonous, that what would be the most trivial pleasure at other times and places, is here magnified into a matter of great importance.
>
> When the hour came for the good dinner, which was known would be provided, hundreds moved upon crutches with feeble, tottering steps to

[81] George Bringhurst to G. Stuart, Tobey Papers, Massachusetts Historical Society.

the table, looking with unmistakable delight upon the display of luxuries. Bands of music enlivened the scene. All the variety of army amusements were permitted and encouraged, followed in the evening by an entertainment of Negro minstrels, – the performers being all white soldiers in the hospital. This last, the soldiers thought the crowning pleasure of the day. At an early hour the large crowds who had enjoyed it all, with the patients, quietly dispersed.[82]

Delegates fondly remembered those days of service at Camp Letterman. One wrote:

The delegates assembled and were enabled to interchange views with each other, and to aid each other as was desirable in the performance of their work. In the regularity of a well-ordered family, the services of the delegates were arranged, and when they met for prayer, or for counsel, or for meals, they experienced the richest satisfaction and enjoyment that the engagements of their Christian pursuits afforded. There is a pleasure in such experience not to be possessed in mansions of ease and elegance and worldly pastime.[83]

ONE UNUSUAL POSTSCRIPT remained. It began just after the battle, when Dr. J. Francis Bourns traveled from Philadelphia to Gettysburg to work as a Christian Commission delegate. While crossing the mountains, Bourns stopped at an inn at Graefenberg Springs, where the owner, Benjamin Schriver, showed them a prize from the battlefield—an ambrotype of three children found in the hands of a dead soldier. There was no other identification on the body.[84]

Dr. Bourns obtained the photograph, determined to find the family. Taking the ambrotype to Philadelphia, he had a local artist reproduce the image for publication. In October, the *Philadelphia Inquirer* ran a story, asking "Whose

---

[82] Anna Holstein, *Three Years in the Field Hospitals in the Army of the Potomac* (Philadelphia: J. B. Lippincott & Co. 1867), 49-54; Gettysburg *Star & Sentinel*, 29 September 1863.

[83] Maryland Committee, *Second Annual Report*, 30.

[84] See Mark H. Dunkelman, *Gettysburg's Unknown Soldier: The Life, Death, and Celebrity of Amos Humiston* (Westport, Connecticut: Praeger, 1999).

Father Was He?" which newpapers throughout the country reprinted. In early November, a copy of the *American Presbyterian*, containing a description of the picture, found its way to Portville, New York, and into the hands of Philinda Humiston, whose husband, Amos, had been missing since the battle of Gettysburg. The description matched that of a photograph sent to her spouse in May. When word filtered back to Bourns, he mailed a carte-de-visite to Portville, then waited for positive identification. As Mrs. Humiston opened the envelope, she saw the image with the faces of her three children, Frank, Alice, and Fred, and knew that she was a widow.

As newspapers retold the touching story, the children became celebrities. Bourns produced copies of the carte-de-visite for sale, using the proceeds to found a home for soldiers' orphans in Gettysburg. It opened in 1866 with Philinda Humiston and her three children in residence.

The Legacy of Gettysburg

No precise statistics show the impact of the Christian Commission at Gettysburg. Their publications often repeated the claim of a medical officer that the work saved at least a thousand lives, although that estimate is based solely on general impressions. In the Central Office in Philadelphia, a folder filled up with letters from grateful individuals. None was more prized than a letter signed by every patient at Camp Letterman, thanking them "for their numberless acts of kindness, for their unsparing contributions, [and] for meeting our dear friends and relatives with an outstretched hand."[85]

Gettysburg secured the United States Christian Commission's reputation as a nationally respected institution, gaining an equivalency with the Sanitary Commission in the public eye. The battlefield, so close to Philadelphia, Baltimore, and New York, provided a perfect opportunity for the "living electric chain" as delegates returned to their homes, full of stories to share. Newspapers carried their anecdotes, gleaned from journals and reports by the Central Office. In the following months, the Commission matched or exceeded the cash donations given to the Sanitary Commission while the number of delegates grew from 191 in 1862 to 1,880 in 1864.

The Sanitary Commission, already uneasy, responded with dismay. Mrs. John Olmsted told Henry Bellows that she regularly heard reports from the front that the "CC went to every bedside, were first on every battlefield." In

[85] USCC, *Second Annual Report*, 86-92.

frustration, Bellows complained to an associate, "It has entered our field…
collecting money and supplies in a way that seriously interferes with our
resources." He bristled at the implied criticism of the Sanitary Commission,
writing, "If at this period of the war our plan & its advantages are not understood & appreciated—it is in vain to argue! we must submit to the popular
verdict—however unjust."[86]

Ironically, just as Gettysburg bolstered the popular image of the Christian
Commission volunteerism, the organization expanded its paid staff. After
the battle, James R. Miller argued forcefully for more professionalism in its
operations.

> We must have one permanent *paid* agent to take charge, and retain it, of
> each station….We want men…who will become efficient businessmen.
> Now our work is unmethodical, and unsystematic. Then it could be
> systematized, and the whole operation would be more thorough and
> efficient.

The Commission adopted this plan in October 1863, swayed by the
argument that an orderly structure enabled better use of volunteers. By the
end of the war, the USCC employed dozens of men and women as salaried
managers. However, unpaid delegates remained at the heart of the work, in
contrast to the largely professional Sanitary Commission.[87]

The experience at Gettysburg convinced the USCC leadership to open
additional avenues of service to women. In early 1864, the Commission
authorized Anne Wittenmyer, a tireless organizer from Iowa, to implement
her plan for special diet kitchens. Located within the major military hospitals,
Wittenmyer employed two hundred salaried women managers to direct staff
that issued more than two million rations over the final year of the war.[88]

At the same time, the Commission organized Ladies' Christian Commissions—auxiliaries to gather funds and donated goods—attempting to match
the extensive Sanitary Commission network of local ladies' aid societies.

[86] Mrs. John Olmsted to Henry W. Bellows, 15 November 1863, Box 955, USSC Papers;
Bellows to Newberry, 10 August 1863, Box 955, USSC Papers.

[87] Smith, "Two Civil War Notebooks of James Russell Miller," 72.

[88] Elizabeth D. Leonard, *Yankee Women: Gender Battles in the Civil War* (New York:
W. W. Norton, 1994), 88-102.

The Executive Committee threw the full weight of the organization into the venture. William Boardman resigned as General Secretary to work solely on the formation of LCC branches, joined by Reverend Bernice Ames, formerly the Home Secretary. Robert Parvin, who directed the Fifth Corps work at Gettysburg, became chairman of the Ladies' Christian Commission with Mrs. William G. Crowell of Philadelphia as Secretary.[89]

The Christian Commission provided a leadership laboratory for the post-war generation of evangelical leaders. James R. Miller, reflecting on the impact of his service, wrote, "Ministers have not know much of life, nor of men. They have in the past been too much confined to their learning to the mere theology of books, and have not stopped to learn from the works of God around, nor from men's hearts and lives—hereafter…men will not confine themselves so closely to the cloister."[90]

After the war, Miller returned to seminary and went on to a distinguished career as a minister and author of dozens of highly popular devotional books. Late in life, he placed a coda on the lessons of Gettysburg in a book of advice to young Christians. He wrote:

> We may not be able to do much to relieve those who are troubled: we certainly cannot work miracles as Christ did; but we may have a heart of love which shall manifest itself toward every one in a spirit of patient gentleness and kindly thoughtfulness.[91]

The men and women carried images and stories from the battlefield that altered their lives. Andrew Cross wrote, "We do not believe that any men or women who labored there regretted the labor and exposure. Many will consider it among the best spent days of their lives."[92] ✢

[89] Moss, *Annals*, 170, 353-354; J. Hamilton to William Boardman, 3 August 1864, USCC Papers, National Archives; "Minutes of the Executive Committee," 2 August 1864, USCC Papers, National Archives.

[90] James Russell Miller Papers, Presbyterian Historical Society.

[91] J. R. Miller, *In His Steps: A Book for Young Christians* (Philadelphia: Westminster Press, 1905), 48.

[92] Cross, *Battle of Gettysburg*, 22

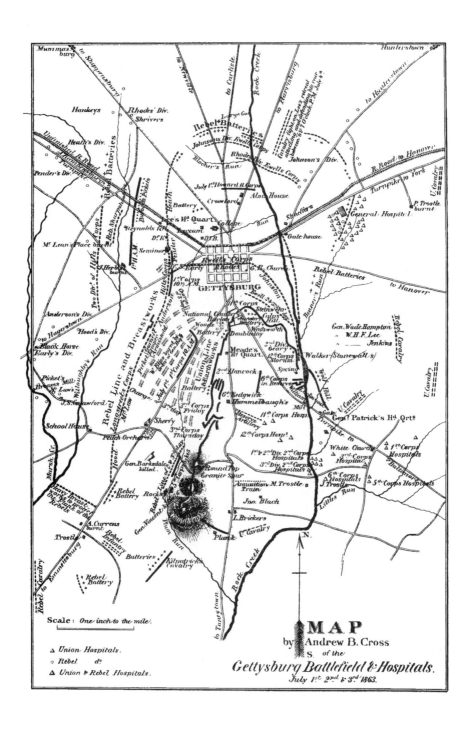

MAP
by Andrew B. Cross
of the
Gettysburg Battlefield & Hospitals.
July 1st 2nd & 3rd 1863.

Scale: One inch to the mile.

△ Union Hospitals.
○ Rebel   do
▲ Union & Rebel Hospitals.

The Battle of Gettysburg
and the Christian Commission

✛ ✛ ✛ ✛ ✛ ✛ ✛

Andrew Boyd Cross

ORN IN 1810, Andrew Cross graduated from the College of New Jersey in
1831, and then attended Princeton Theological Seminary. Shortly after
ordination by the Presbyterian Church, Cross co-founded and served as
Associate Editor of *The Baltimore Literary and Religious Magazine*. One contemporary said, "The articles by Mr. Cross were distinguished by marked
ability." A prolific writer, his books included *Priest's Prisons for Women*, an
anti-Catholic treatise, *The Street Preacher*, and *Woman: Man's Help-Meet*.[1]

Following a stint as pastor of the Bethel Church in Harford County,
Maryland, Cross turned his attention to temperance reform, editing the
Maryland *Temperance Herald* from 1845-1849, and acting as Corresponding
Secretary and Agent for the Maryland Temperance Society. His advocacy of
temperance, anti-romanism, and anti-slavery views contributed to the rise
of the American Party in Maryland in the 1850s. He filled ministerial posts
in several Maryland churches in addition to his writing career.[2]

When the war broke out, Cross volunteered with the Maryland Committee
of the Christian Commission. One of the first delegates to reach Gettysburg,
he rode north from Baltimore on the top of a railroad car on July 4. He was
fifty-two at the time. He remained at the hospitals through the fall of 1863,
generally working among wounded Confederates at the Lutheran Seminary.
His report, *The Battle of Gettysburg and the Christian Commission*, is the most

---

[1] *Priest's Prisons for Women* (Baltimore: Sherwood & Co., 1854), *The Street Preacher*
(Baltimore: Sherwood & Co., 1860), and *Woman: Man's Help-Meet* (Baltimore:
Sherwood & Co., 1867).

[2] Jean Baker, *Ambivalent Americans: The Know-Nothing Party in Maryland* (Baltimore:
Johns Hopkins University Press, 1977), 137-139.

complete contemporary description of the organization's work at Gettysburg. Written to encourage public support, he closes with a passionate appeal for donations, stating, "These men were your fathers, husbands, brothers and sons. Do you grudge the help they received?"

Cross worked almost continuously until the war's conclusion, first at Point Lookout Hospital, Maryland, and then at City Point, Virginia, just outside of Petersburg. The following year he contributed a similar report, *The War and the Christian Commission*, covering its work through 1864.

After the war, Cross devoted his time to the development of new churches and Sunday Schools in the Baltimore area. "A decided friend of Negro education," as one biographer noted, Cross was a Trustee of Lincoln University in Virginia for many years. He died in 1889.[3]

THE BATTLE OF GETTYSBURG on July 1, 2, 3, 1863, if not the Waterloo of the war, taught the Rebel arms that there is a limit which they cannot pass. Our children when reading its history will be able clearly to see the hand of God giving order and position to our forces, putting honor on the acknowledgment of dependence upon Him, driving back the destructive elements of rebellion, which had acquired such force, advanced with such rapidity and confident daring, as to make the adjacent population, and, indeed, all from the Potomac north and east to tremble.

It will be the part of engineers to give accurate accounts of the plan of battle, the amount of ordinance and ammunition for the surgeons to report the number of killed and wounded, the nature of their wounds, the amputation of limbs, their successes, and the many instances of hope and disappointment in most promising cases.

Each department, corps, division, brigade, regiment, company, will feel interested in recording its contest and success, while sadness will fill all who look into the record, at the remembrance of the loss of life, and the severe and protracted suffering of the maimed ones who still live.

[3] Committee of the Association, *Necrological Reports and Annual Proceedings of the Alumni Association of Princeton Theological Seminary*, Vol. II, 1890-1899 (Princeton: C. S. Robinson, 1899), 27-28; Alfred Nevin, editor, *Encyclopaedia of the Presbyterian Church in the United States of America* (Philadelphia, Presbyterian Encyclopaedia Publishing Co., 1884), 166.

There are others who will feel all interest in its history. The wife will read and examine to see if there be any trace by which she call fix her mind upon the spot where the bones of him whom she loved—the mother who mourns over the son of her heart and hope of her life, and the children as they grow up will retain the hope, that some day their father may come home from the war; they will read and examine these particular presentations, cherishing a hope that something may turn up by which they call be identified with him, while they with sorrow remember the last day when they saw him go out front his door—when he kissed them, and bade them that long farewell.

No pen shall write out those histories—no heart can enter into and be made fully to partake of those varied and unmingled sorrows, which identify so many thousand hearts, with the hills and fields, the rocky places, the swamps the houses and barns around the lines of that terrible battle. Like the roll of the prophet, it must be written within and without, with lamentations and mourning and woe.

Our object is chiefly to present all account of the aims and efforts of the Christian Commission in ministering to the wounded and dying, whether left on the battle-field, in the hospitals, in the tents, barns, woods, sheds, houses, college, seminary, school-houses, court-house, churches, &c., &c.

Cross' original text described the battle, placing emphasis on God's hand in the events. The narrative resumes with a history of the work of the Christian Commission.

A battle on which was virtually to turn the peace, quiet, and safety of the States of Pennsylvania, Maryland, Delaware, New Jersey, &c.; which was also to shape the character of the remaining conflict of the war; which was fought to compel recognition and terms of submission on the part of the Government and local States, and which, according to General Lee's report, "became a necessity for the existence of his army where it was," must be one of desperation.—So when on the afternoon of Friday the clangor of arms ceased, and men began to look at the field, and during that night, the next day, and on to Sabbath morning, to gather up the dead and wounded, it became evident that a slaughter, fearful and unparalleled, had taken place. Some put down the Union loss in killed at about 2,500, and over 12,000 wounded. The Rebel loss in killed must have been much heavier, while the number of their wounded must have been still greater in proportion. General Lee says "his army were driven back with *severe loss.*"

There are a number of circumstances connected with the two armies' which might be noted. Gen. Meade was placed in command, Sabbath, June 28. His officers and men scarcely knew of him. He had never fought a battle as commander. His men were marched continuously and rapidly from 150 to 200 miles. They were hurried into the battle, many of them with very little food; some without shoes, tired and lame. It was a position or trial to the commander and his army. Gen. Lee was experienced; had fought all the battles of the Army of Northern Virginia; in many of them very successful. His army were elated at former successes; felt themselves invincible; had every confidence in their commander. He felt that he could rely upon them to attempt anything he would propose. His men were rested and well fed, and probably double ours in number. The ground upon which we would have fought lay west of Gettysburg, our army seeking to possess themselves of the Seminary hill and that ridge. The defeat of the first day compelled them to take the position which, in the Providence of God, enabled them to stand, and which was four times as good a position for defence, so that we may consider the defeat and loss of the first day, that which seemed is a defence on the second, and victory on the third; but that was probably the result of the 6th Corps under Sedgwick coming up just when our lines were trembling, and ready to give way.

It is wonderful that so heavy a battle should take place in and around a town, and do so little damage to life or property as in Gettysburg. Shells fell in the yard and went through the house of Mr. *Little* and exploded in the very room where a few minutes before, his family had been sitting. A shell, unexploded, is lodged in a wall of a brick house, over the door of the third house east of the town square. A shell went through the corner of a house on the same street. The house of Mr. *Stuck*, which was a rendezvous of Rebel sharpshooters, has shell upon shell through it, and nearly every square foot upon the side next Cemetery hill has the mark of a bullet. About two persons was the limit of lives of the citizens lost, so far as we could learn. The house known as Dr. McLean's, west of the Seminary, was set fire to and burned by the Rebels, supposed in mere wantonness.

General Meade took charge of the army, recognizing the controlling Providence of God. After the battle he said to his army: "*It is right and proper to return thanks to the Almighty Disposer of events, that in the goodness of his Providence he has thought fit to give victory to the cause of the just.*"–Head-quarters, July 4, 1863.

When the Union Army moved from the Potomac to meet Lee, such expedition was needed that it required a dispensing with everything which could be left. Rations were only for a few days. Its supplies, which were in Alexandria, Washington, &c., had to come through Baltimore, by the N.C.R.R., to the Relay House, up the Western Maryland Railroad to Union bridge, it being the nearest point to the army. Then as it advanced, Westminster became the base from which everything had to be wagoned. Provision was needed for the whole army, which was hurrying up, not knowing where they might meet the enemy, but assured that wherever they met must be a terrific battle. Supplies had to come for man and beast; from delays they became more urgent. An immense pressure was upon cars, wagons, ambulances or whatever could carry freight.

Our Commission first sent supplies to Frederick. As the armies advanced, we looked for them to meet about Saturday, the 6th, near the Union bridge or Emmittsburg. We made our arrangements on the 2d to go by Westminster. That day the announcement was made that there had been an engagement near Gettysburg, and General Reynolds killed; that appearances were unfavorable for our army. Everything looked gloomy, but there was no time to delay. We immediately got our stores in readiness to start. On calling upon Colonel Donaldson, the Quartermaster in Baltimore, he readily and promptly gave us what facility he could, as well as advice. He would have furnished a wagon and ambulances to take our goods to the battlefield, but from depredations of guerillas and Stuart's cavalry, advised us not to take that way, but the military road, which was the railroad to Westminister. He gave us an order on the railroad President and Superintendent. Messrs. Dubarry and Irvine promptly gave us the facilities on their roads, free.—We had our goods sent to the Calvert Station, then re-shipped at the Relay, and that evening placed in a car with General Meade's mail for Westminster or the army. After we had secured them in the cars at the Relay at 10 o'clock at night, we had to wait for a train, walking the platform or sitting about the car, until 7 o'clock the next morning. We were so fortunate before the train started as to get some breakfast through the kindness of Mrs. Samuel Barnes. We first entered a burden car, but soon found it would be more comfortable, though a little more dangerous, on the top. Tired of walking all night, and anxious to get on in any way, the top of the car became quite comfortable. We arrived at Westminster at noon Saturday. Just as we landed there was a report that General Buford's cavalry were ordered off, as some supposed, to head Lee's army, or to bring up some aid to General Meade. No one knew with any certainty.

At Westminster, everything was in the utmost confusion. Dozens of men were loading hard crackers; others meat and sugar, &c. from cars into army wagons, which, as soon as loaded, were hurried away for the army, which was not supplied. A little farther along the track, under guard, stood about 1,000 Confederate prisoners, waiting to enter the cars for Baltimore. Several hundred of our wounded had reached here and were attended to by our delegates. General Hancock, of the 2d Army Corps, who was wounded on the 2d day, was here, and had his wound dressed and the smoke and dust of the battle washed from him by one of our Commission (Mr. Stilson). From him we learned positively that our army was victorious. General Buford had ordered an army wagon to take our supplies, which we immediately had removed from the car to the wagon. While in this work, and just as we had nearly finished, one or two cavalry men rode up to us, inquiring which was the road to some stone church? In a few moments there was a new commotion. Wagons, horses and footmen were hurrying along.–We sought to know what this meant, and were informed that General Buford's cavalry was in motion. In a moment there came wagons, with 6 mules at a trot, followed by ammunition wagons, men on horseback, ambulances &c., everything in the line making their way with great expedition, no one being able to say where. Some said it was a call for reinforcements, others a retreat of our army. Feeling that we were shut up to the duty of reaching the wounded, we pursued the steps to accomplish it. A proposition was made to hire a carriage. Knowing what difficulty we had in getting our stores that far, we concluded to stick by the wagon, while others went in a carriage, and as we knew from General Hancock how great was the need in the army, we resolved to go with it at once. Just as we were about starting, a cloud suddenly arose, which, with great rapidity, gave evidence of a severe storm. In a few moments it was upon us in torrents. Umbrellas and wagon covers were of but little use. We fled to a house and after waiting until the first furious shower had slackened a little, we started. It continued raining until about 5 o'clock. We pressed on through mud and rain and over the rough, stony and hilly roads to Taneytown. While our horses were eating, we called at the house of our friend, Rev. Mr. Scarborough, the Presbyterian preacher in that place, whose good wife insisted on giving us some supper, adding to our stores some loaves of bread. Soon as our horses were done eating, we

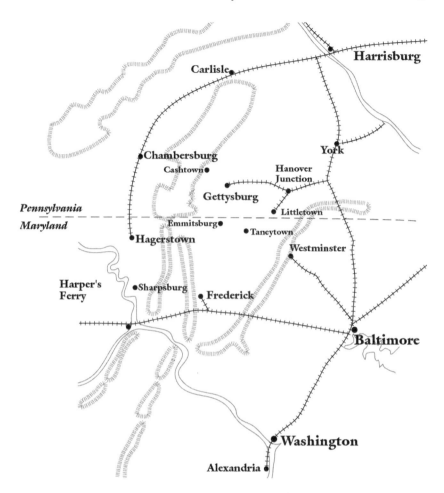

urged our driver to start. He soon began to falter and make excuses to stop
for the night. Presently a sound of horses' feet, which proved to be cavalry
guarding the beef cattle of General Meade's army, aroused him sufficiently
to journey on as long as they were in hearing. Very soon after he turned into
a field where were three ambulances spending in the night. Here we waited
until daylight, when we had to put our wits to work to get him off without
waiting for his breakfast. As he had two days allowed him in which to make
his trip, we told him if he would get us to the hospital of the 2d Army corps,
he might do what he pleased with the rest of the time by which and urging
the condition of wounded men, we induced him to start.

The heavy rain of the preceding day continued through the night and
morning. The immense wagoning which had been upon this clay road,

made it difficult to get along, even by going through the fields, and would have been utterly impossible in the night. Very soon we came to squads of soldiers who had wandered off six to eight miles to see what they could obtain at the farm houses along the road; then along the road and in the field we could see dead horses, who, after being wounded, had probably fled as far as they could, and there had dropped down and died. From daylight we noticed companies of cavalry turning in all the roads leading west from the Taneytown road. Since we learned they were searching for the whereabouts of Lee's army, which that morning had moved in retreat. As we advanced toward the round top, General Meade's extreme left, we came upon a portion of the 5th and 6th corps of Sykes and Sedgwick. These were scattered in every direction, in houses, barns and trees, &c. Here were wagons, tents, stacks of guns, here a little fire, there a few men trying to keep on a place where they would not be in water or mud. One would inquire of its how many of the militia were out? Another, whether General McClellan was not in command of them? This part of the army did not know that the battle was over. With a knowledge of the severity of the preceding day's fight, it was very natural to be anxious for reinforcements. Many were in waiting for orders to renew the fight.

We inquired for the 2d corps hospital, but no one could tell. One said, in this barn, another in that, but none knew. Seeing at a distance a train of about 30 to 40 ambulances coming from the battlefield, we made our way to them, and learned that they were going to the 2d corps. Beckoning to our driver, we followed them, and in short time reached the hospital of the 3d division of this corps. These troops were the extreme left, and the 2d corps was near the centre, which accounts for their not knowing about it, they all being strangers in the neighborhood, and having been hard at work from the time they came up. This hospital was about 2 to 2 1/2 miles from the lines on our right, in a woods and along Rock Creek. The ground for this division was very unfavorable, being flat, muddy and wet.

Some little idea of the condition of this hospital and the destruction of the battle may be inferred from the fact that there were over 3,200 wounded in all, living, besides many dead lying around it, 2,308 Union and 952 Rebels; 245 of the Union men died and 192 Rebels; in all 437, being about one-ninth of our men and one-fifth of the Rebels. These men were more severely wounded and more enfeebled and exhausted.

We came into the midst of these wounded and dying and dead, as they were lying on the ground and being lifted from ambulances and laid beside others who were on the ground, without anything under or over them. Many had lost nearly all their clothes in the fight; others when wounded had to have their clothes torn off to stop the blood and attend to their wounds. We proposed to go to the battlefield to help gather up the wounded, dying and dead, but were informed that it would not be allowed as the Rebel sharpshooters were still hidden about, and would fire upon any person that would come beyond a certain line, or unless connected with the ambulances; that the day before a Confederate officer had offered $500 to an ambulance driver if he would get him off the field. The Rebel commander kept these sharpshooters to annoy our ambulance drivers, and keep our army from the knowledge of his defeat and retreat. Some men in places had thus to lay on the ground a day and a half longer than there was any necessity.

The rain not only made the ground at this division hospital muddy, but at time so overflowed, that some of the wounded were drowned for want of help to move them from the low and flat places; at times it was with difficulty we could walk through the hospital. There were few tents, some little shelter coverings, some gum cloths spread on two rails, with any cloth or covering they could get, but the great mass had no cover or shelter. Some with a pair of pants and no shirt, some a pair of drawers; the scarcity of everything was exceedingly great, no army provisions of any kind having yet come, and the men having been without food in many cases for three days.

When the wagon came up the surgeons and men received us with the greatest gladness. Each would ask,–Have you any bandages, lint, sheets, blankets, &c.? We are in want of everything. So, of wines, bread, &c. We said to them, we have some of all these, and they are at your service at once. But what were they among such a multitude?

To make everything go as far as possible, we resolved to let nothing out but through one of our agents, and then only to extreme cases, as where a man had a leg or arm amputated, or was exhausted by his wounds and exposure. Painful as it was, the necessity was upon us, and we must do the best we could. Borrowing the horse of Dr. Scott, of the 7th Virginia and putting one of our Commission in charge of our goods, and procuring him a guard, we hastened to the 3d and 5th corps hospitals. On inquiry of the Surgeons, the question was immediate,–Have you any lint, bandages, sponges, stimulants &c.? We directed each of them to send over, and we would do for them what we could. Coming back, the necessity for economy became so terrible that when a poor fellow, who had periled his life for his country, and had a wounded arm or leg, begged for bread, we were often compelled to break a soda cracker in two, give him half, and the remainder to another wounded in his foot or leg.

While we were distributing from man to man, the men came from the 3d and 5th corps, when we had to divide our goods into three parts, giving one to each of them. Think of two boxes of soda crackers in hospital of over 3,000 wounded men who had not anything to eat for three days! But what when divided among hospitals of three corps? It was all that we had, and no appearance of supply from any other quarter. As we cut up a loaf of bread, which we had gotten at Mr. Scarborough's to give it to those who had been wounded about the mouth and face, who could not chew a cracker, a man standing by begged us to sell him a slice of it. He would pay any price. How like Job's account: "All that a man hath will he give for his life."–2, 4. But to him we could only say, "We can't sell it to you at any price. We would gladly give it to you, but look at those men around you; say whether we ought to let you have it?" "It's all right; give it to them." These men felt their gnawing hunger and wounds, but when they saw the condition of their companions they readily yielded.

The first two men we supplied were of 125th and 111th New York, the next two of 21st North Carolina, then 11th U. S. Infantry, an ambulance officer, then a Chaplain of 14th Connecticut, and Rev. Messrs. [Jonathan] Adams, [George] Chapin &c., of the Christian Commission for distribution. In a fence corner just above us, among our men, lay Colonel Hugh R. Miller, of Pontotoc, Mississippi, of the 42d Mississippi Regiment, an eminent lawyer and judge of that State, shot through the left breast and right knee. We gave him a little wine and a cracker, which he took with great modesty, saying he was not dangerously wounded, but was thankful for our offer to write to his wife, Mrs. Susan G. Miller at Sunnyside, Cumberland Co., Virginia. The Surgeon told us his case was dangerous. Calling again after a short time to see if he would have anything, he modestly said: "I am very much obliged to you, but give it to those around who are worse, and need it more." On the 20th we met his son in the office of Colonel Alleman, stating that his father was dead, and requesting liberty to accompany his body home.

A full description of the condition of the wounded would require the attention of one who was not so much occupied in getting the things needed

Jonathan Edwards Adams
Adams directed the Commission's
station in the Second Corps Hospital,
Third Division. Azor Howett Nickerson
called him "a real hero of Gettysburg."

by them and those of other corps. We can say, however, that in every direction lay men of all classes, the rich man and the poor man, the commander and the private. At one place, near a fence, lay privates, corporals, lieutenants, majors and colonels, from New York, North Carolina, Indiana, Mississippi, Connecticut, Georgia, New Hampshire, Alabama, Maine, and Delaware, side by side, on the bare ground, or on a little wet straw; no distinction. Men were gathered around trees with their heads toward the body of the tree; occasionally, when able, one sat up and leaned against it. They were in every condition, from the slightest wound to the man dying in agony, from the terrible mangling of a piece of shell.

To say in such a field that surgeons were busy, is needless. What else could they do but work, unless appalled at the mass of ragged, naked, torn, and mangled mortality! There was not more than one for ten that were needed. Every man that could tie a bandage, or give a drink of water, or pour it upon a wound, was at work. As we passed through them, in every direction we turned, men would call us. "Doctor, oh, doctor, won't you attend to my case? Won't you fix my arm, or my leg, or my shoulder, or head?" As we stopped at their earnest cries we could only say, we are not physicians or surgeons, but acting for the Christian Commission and will do for you what we can. Until the Dr. can attend to your case, we will furnish you with some wine, biscuit, crackers, bandages, lint, shirts, &c. They would then beg us to send the Dr.; but to whom could we go? On the amputation table one case succeeded another as fast as they could be operated on and removed. We little thought we could become so familiar with the sight of feet, legs, arms, just taken from our fellow-men and look upon the operations without a thought except the inclination to take hold of the man and try and help him. During all this time, Mr. Stilson and myself had never thought of eating, having forgotten breakfast, when a man told us *Dr. Scott* had some dinner prepared for us. His name was *Lewis Morgan*, Delaware, Delaware county, Ohio, Co. 1, 4th Ohio. His kind, pleasant, and attentive manners left all impression on us not soon to be forgotten. Dr. Scott detailed him to attend us. After we went to the town, the Commission found him the same.

While giving out to the men, we noticed at the table a man whom we had been supplying to give to others, who looked like a chaplain. We were old acquaintances and knew each other well, but during the day, meeting time and again at the same boxes, had never recognized each other. As we turned up to straighten our back, after getting things out, we recognized him. "Well, Murphy where in the world did you come from? I have been here all day, never noticed you before." "I am chaplain of the 1st Delaware, and am here attending to the wounded of my regiment." We said this was new work for two such old fashioned Presbyterians, to be hard at work in boxes and bread, &c., on the Sabbath day. "What," said he, "is it the Sabbath day?" Indeed, I had not the least idea what day it was. I can't tell anything about where I am, or what time has passed for three or four days." We said that when day broke we recognized the Sabbath, but from that until the present we had not thought of anything but these goods, and to get them to the men that needed them, not had it ever entered into our mind where we were. This was the first Sabbath we ever recollect spending in bodily labor or secular; but when the exception of necessity and mercy takes place, the exception becomes the duty.

As soon as we had eaten, we started to try some plan to get more surgeons, but were stopped by a report that any private surgeons were forbidden on the field. Just then Dr. Scott said he and all the surgeons that could in any way be spared were ordered forward with the army, which would be or was in motion. What! take away surgeons here where a hundred are wanted, and where, if the men have not immediate help, hundreds must die for want of that attention. But so it is, and we can do no better.

As Dr. Scott was ordered off, we had to try and get another horse. After searching, we found a wounded officer, who had a horse—Major Richard E. Cross, of the 5th New Hampshire (brother of Col. Edward E. Cross, who was killed on the 3d day) both formerly of Baltimore. He loaned it to us to go into Gettysburg and see if we could not make some arrangement for surgeons and supplies, but wanted it in the morning as he was going to try and keep up with the army. When at Westminster we had written to Mr. Griffith, chairman of Commission, not to send any more supplies by that way. Knowing the communication by Northern Central Railroad, Hanover, and Gettysburg, we started to see the President of Gettysburg Road, hoping to be able to do something in the way of facilitating supplies. On our arrival at the cross road on the turnpike a mile south of the Cemetery hill, we were stopped by a guard. We went down the turnpike a mile further where Gen. Meade then had his headquarters to state our case and get passed. Col. Sharp said we would have to go to Gen. Patrick's headquarters, which were nearly two miles further. It was now after 9 o'clock, damp and dark, at that. To comfort us, he said he would go along and let us share his bed, which was on the barn floor, near the 3d Corps hospital, as far from the town as from where we had started. The General ordered the pass, preferred we should go in town, but on our remonstrating as we were from Baltimore, had brought supplies for the wounded, and had been all day on out, feet in water and mud distributing them, he said we might lodge in the barn with him; that these people around here he could not trust. Col. Sharp having ordered some one to tie up our horse, we laid down on the barn floor, where we slept more soundly than we have often done in the most comfortable bed. At daylight we were off to Gettysburg, where we saw *Mr. McCurdy*, the president of the railroad, and learned that the Government had the road in hand; that cars would be up as soon as they could have the road ready. We went to the Seminary and College hospitals, and around the town, in court house, churches, &c., where we found a continued specimen of what we had down the country, only that they were sheltered and dry, and had some attendants.

When we left the corps hospital, the cry began to be heard, "Bread! bread!" We did not know where to turn to get it. After we came to the town, as we came down from one of the hospitals in the town, we espied a wagon with bread, &c. We hailed the man to lay violent hands on it, to send down to the hospital, when he told us that it was in charge of Mr. Latimer Small, of York, who had passed us, but a moment before, in a carriage with some other persons. We hurried up to him, learned there was more coming and urged him to send it to the 3d division of 2d corps. He gave direction, and afterwards we heard of the joy which it gave many wounded men.

We had been directed to make headquarters at the 2d Army corps, but we at once saw that it was not the place. The town was full of hospitals, and east, north and west of the town Rebel hospitals, among which were many of our own wounded. We rode back to the 2d corps, left the horse, and came to the town. Here we met with other members of the Commission, and united in securing *Mr. S[c]hick's* store for reception of goods, which were coming to the Commission from citizens around York, Hanover, Carlisle, Lancaster, Baltimore, Philadelphia, &c., and indeed from almost every direction. But a few days before they were in dread of the invading army, now with grateful hearts and willing hands, they were bringing of what had been saved, and offering it to supply food and clothing for the wounded, who had borne the burden of their defence. It was a proper tribute, and the abundance which so overflowed the large store-room from day to day, and required the securing of another on the opposite corner, showed that it was without stint. This was renewed from day to day and through our Commission delegates, we had these daily supplies immediately distributed. The hospitals in and about the town had received of what the citizens could give. Those in the country were the 1st, 2nd, 3d, 5th, 6th, 11th, 12th corps, and the demand was enormous. The whole hospital demands seemed for days to fall on the Commission for every kind of things needed. It is not a small tribute that came from surgeons, nurses, wounded, among our own army and the Rebels: "We do not know what we would have done if it had not been for the Christian Commission." Our rooms were no sooner opened and underway than the demand also of *the hospitals of the town* were added—the College, Seminary, Court House, Public School House, Lutheran, Presbyterian, Catholic and United Presbyterian Churches, hotels, warehouses, private houses, depots, and tents almost everywhere. There were, in addition, twenty-five to thirty Confederate hospitals, in barns, in stables, corn sheds, dwelling houses, taverns, mills, in woods, in tents, &c., from 1 1/2 miles to 7 and 8 off the town. The town was emptied of food by the Rebels, and by the supply which the people had furnished the wounded.

Our wounded of the 2d and 3d days were generally taken to barns, houses, sheds, tents, &c. wherever they could get them along the borders of Rock creek, where they would be out of the way of danger. Those after the battle left on the field were taken, whether our own or Rebels, to the Corps hospitals, which swelled their number. Those of ours which had fallen in the Rebel lines on Wednesday and Thursday, in common with their own, were taken to the hospitals which were in the field held by them, as Seminary, College, &c., in town and in barns along Marsh creek, on the Hagerstown, Chambersburg, Shippensburg, Carlisle and Hunterstown roads. Marsh creek and Rock creek are head tributaries of the Monocacy, and run on opposite sides of Gettysburg. The surface of the country around is broken; the weather was wet, roads muddy, conveyances held at extortionate prices, and almost impossible to procure, and everything in demand at the same rate. To get at these different hospitals was no little work, and then to get goods to them would have been impossible, but through the kindness and promptness of Col. Rankin, quartermaster, who furnished us wagons and ambulances on call, and thus enabled us daily to send out wagon loads to the different hospitals. The amount of labor required in the mere receiving, opening, unpacking, distributing, and then arranging and sending out, is incredible. The Commission depot seemed for two weeks to be the headquarters of everything connected with the wants and supply for the tens of thousands of wounded and dying and never did men work more industriously and perseveringly. From daylight until midnight every day would be found Messrs. Shearer, Williams, McCreary, Mill[e]r, Woodward, and others, receiving, assorting, supplying demands, &c.

It was often amusing to see the delegates that came in from each of these hospitals daily to receive such supplies as were needed. A mother could not have been more anxious for the supply to her children than these men were to procure whatever would make comfortable the wounded in their particular district. Our plan was to have one of our delegates come in from each hospital daily with a list of the wants at that place, immediately have them assorted, arranged and sent out; he accompanying them. When arrived at the hospital, there it would be subdivided or distributed from our tent as each delegate came or sent for any individual in need. In this way we tried to reach every man, and know that he received it.

Goods that came to our Commission, we did not allow to remain in our boxes and barrels, or on our shelves, or in our tents, waiting the requisition of Surgeons. We had not learned the *red tapeism* which would suffer a patient to starve to death, while the goods rotted on hand, waiting for those requisitions to come in the name and on the behalf of men who had no one to attend to them or speak to them; men who had neither pen, ink, paper, or a hand with which to write their need. Just such an institution as the Commission *was a necessity.*

We do not speak disparagingly, but what we saw and know, when we say that no body of men could have done more prompt and effective service. From 300 to 400 men, hurried away from their homes, regardless of weather or situation, looking only to be able to render service which might comfort or alleviate the condition of the wounded. The fact that he was a wounded man, was generally enough to call for their services. Occasionally the patriotic zeal of some of our delegates and friends would deter them from attending to the Rebels. Some felt that they ought not to help them, but generally, without reserve, they adopted the principle of the Gospel, which says: "*If thine enemy hunger, feed him,*" *&c.*–Rom. xxi: 19-21; Prov. xxv: 21.

On the morning of Monday 6th, going through the College hospital, almost entirely filled with Rebel wounded, a young, pleasant-faced lad asked us rather anxiously for food. He had not had a meal from Tuesday before, six days. We told him of the difficulty of supply from the burning of the railroad bridges, that our own were in the same condition; that, as soon as we could receive, they should be supplied. With earnestness he said: "*Didn't Stuart burn them? So he makes his own men suffer as well as others.*" Passing through a room on the north of the building, on the first floor, we saw about sixteen, lying on the floor, all badly wounded, several of whom died. They looked anxiously for something to eat. We tried to encourage them in the hope of help the next day. When at the door turning round, we said we had a few dried apples, which we were chewing for our own dinner. They were nothing comparatively, and were so few that we felt ashamed to offer them, and did not expect them to go around one a piece, but as in our haste we threw them, without thought of their wounds, every man exerted himself to catch. There happened to be just one apiece for them, and never did we see men enjoy a little thing more. In a few days, help came. Immense as the demand, the quantity was renewed and increased day by day. We felt for once in our lives that there was a spring in the hearts of the people which had never before been well tried. It was like in the building of the temple, when the people had to be bidden not to send any more.

It is but proper to say that other organizations, especially the Adams Express and the Sanitary Commission, after they commenced, did great and effective service in the abundance of their supplies. After a time, all these, except the Christian and Sanitary Commission, left. These have remained until the present, and the Christian Commission has efficiently and constantly continued its supply of delicacies, &c., while it has endeavored, by all the help it could use, to speak words of comfort and consolation to the sick and dying and keep up the preaching of the Gospel to the wounded with regular religious services.

As the men at the different hospitals became fit for removal, they were sent away to hospitals in different parts of Maryland and Pennsylvania, and District of Columbia. Then a *general hospital* was established near the town, about 1 1/4 miles east, on the York turnpike, while the Seminary was also retained. The general hospital of tents was in a very excellent situation, a beautiful spot, with a skirt of woods on north-east and also on south-west, a good spring of water very near, the ground gradually rolling so that water did not remain after a rain.

There were from 125 to 150 tents. Those for the wounded were large, well-built and capable of containing comfortably from twelve to sixteen persons, were on good bedsteads with mattresses. The arrangements were such as to make everything convenient; so much so that, after observing those in tents and such as were in our large and well-constructed buildings, we were fully persuaded that the tents, until severely cold weather, were the most healthy and convenient for the patients, and as convenient for surgeons and nurses.

The Rev. Mr. Sloan, who was on the ground among the first of our men, remained attending at the Seminary and cases in town until the hospital at Seminary was removed.

The removing was in ambulances when the men could bear the ride. When it was a bad case, they were placed on stretchers, or their bed and carried by four men.

At the general hospital, we had our tents and delegates, continuing from the commencement of the encampment to its close. The labors here were more systematic and regular, because we had gotten things into one place and under regular order. The services of ministers and laymen from different denominations, were here rendered with diligence and fidelity. Among others, the Rev. George Junkin, D. D., spent 19 days of untiring labor, talking to, exhorting and praying with the men. Though so warm a Union man, the Rebel wounded were very much interested in hearing him, from the fact that he was the father-in-law of General T. J. (Stonewall) Jackson.

The effect has not been lost. Our own men thanked us; our enemies wonder while they acknowledged the kindness. Daily in our places of distribution, and where we met them, they expressed their gratitude: "They did not expect to be treated in this way." "We are not afraid of your iron balls and

George Junkin
President of Lafayette College,
Easton, Pennsylvania, and father of
Stonewall Jackson's first wife.

heavy cannon"—said they—"but we can't stand this." The eyes of the men
sparkled with joy in the reception of these kindnesses. In our hearing, two
officers remarked, others around assenting, *"This treatment will perfectly
subjugate us."* They speak of its effects in producing the most happy results,
not only in the benefit to their wounded, but in the tendency which it will
have yet to bind us together.

While we have given attention to the Rebel wounded, our own have in no
case been neglected. They have been ministered to with a sumptuousness in
goods and a devotedness of labor which could not but make them realize that
everything which it was in the power of their friends to do had been done
to alleviate their sorrow. That they are grateful, it is not necessary to have
answered by word of month, their beaming countenances and the joy with
which they greeted us abundantly answered.

It is not out of place to say that the wounded of both armies are greatly
debtors to the kind care and generosity of thousands of individuals, who
have furnished the varieties of little comforts of every kind. So it will be
gratifying to those who have contributed to know that their gifts have been
sown with a broad cast, which has left them in the keeping of many hearts
all over the country.

For example, on Sabbath morning, July 5, a box was opened, in which was
the following note:

Thompson, Conn., June 2, 1863

Mr. Rowland:—We send you this box for the soldiers, from the Benevolent Society of East Thompson, consisting of 6 shirts, 12 pairs of stockings, 3 napkins and 402 yards of bandages.

Please send a receipt, and direct to Webster, Mass. Yours,

Mrs. Medora Kemp

It is possible these ladies may have doubted sometimes whether they were not laboring in vain; that this little box would never be heard of. But never was a cup of cold water given to a sick or dying man more desirable or appropriate. With my own hands I knocked open the box on that Sabbath. In the midst of our hurry I read the note, remarking to myself, these ladies ought to know the value of that box; that it was not only received but opened and used at the time when the greatest demand existed for the above articles that ever had been in this country. The half dozen shirts went to men from Indiana, Ohio, Pennsylvania, New Jersey, Delaware, and New Hampshire. The stockings to more than twelve men, because in a number of cases they were given, and always first to men who had one foot amputated. The bandages may have been appropriated to men from twenty States.

The very same thing which occurred in this case, happened daily in almost every box received. The persons getting them up had no idea who shall be the receiver. Sometimes it might happen that the clothes would be put upon the child of her who prepared them a thousand miles from his home, and the delicacies which allay, sweeten and comfort, in the midst of war's calamities, the suffering and dying man, may have been prepared by the hand of a mother or sister. But aside from such incidents they minister to the joy of one who has periled his life for his men. They are given to wounded, sick and dying men.

An effort was made on the part of those dispensing and scattering to turn everything to the very best account. The success of the labors of those who have at this time been disposing of these goods has been such as to make all who have any heart in the work rejoice in the favor conferred upon them in being permitted to minister them.

We have heard many of both sides say that such actions as our Commission will do more to put an end to the war and make us live in peace and harmony under the Union than anything else. There is a time and a presence recorded in the Gospel when the disciples of Jesus said: "It is good to be here." So I must say, in distributing, arranging, and using up among all parties these various gifts, and in beholding the joys and comforts afforded to the receiver, it is a pleasure to the person who is permitted to confer the favor often times as much, if not more, than to the recipient. The promptness, cordiality and earnestness with which men came to labor and the readiness with which they said, "send me where you most need me," and the will with which they worked, was very gratifying.

Some one inquired of General Scott at the commencement of the war, if the barbarity of uncivilized nations should not be eschewed. He said that it should be conducted "*on Christian principles*," meaning that Christianity should modify every unnecessary cruelty and suffering. He did not mean by this that there should grow up an organization which would bring all the principles of the Gospel to bear upon the sick, wounded and dying soldier in a private way, but that the officers and soldiers and the opposing powers should carry it on as nearly as possible in accordance with the light and influence which Christianity has exercised upon the present generation.

To nothing, however, which has happened can his remarks be so truly applied as to the object and action of the Christian Commission. It was organized to aid our own soldiers. It sought to bring those delicacies and light food to the sick and dying soldier which he would have had at home in his sickness. It tries to make him remember his home and his country. But it also comes to keep in his remembrance the Christian principles in which he has been educated, to encourage him, and throw around him a safeguard in the way of temptation, to point him to Jesus, the Savior of sinners, comfort and console him in the hour of death.

Probably no institution has, during the same period of time, done as much in the way of religious influence. We shall not speak of other battles, armies, hospitals, or of its influence on our navy. We speak with reference to its influence at Gettysburg and vicinity since the battle.

The amount of stores, consisting of all under clothing, comforts, blankets, sheets, lint and sponges, &c., &c., to make comfortable as possible the suffering body; then the dried and preserved fruit in every form; stimulants of wines and brandies, &c.; the home-made wines and cordials, fresh bread, crackers, toasted rusk, cornstarch, farina, sage, coffee, tea, sugar, oranges, lemons, ice, &c., with almost every kind of thing that could be procured, to an immense amount, was daily furnished to and distributed by the delegates of the Commission. Gentlemen and ladies of wealth and standing, ministers of the Gospel, surgeons and laymen, with a freeness and heartiness, laid aside all the formalities of position, and worked indefatigably in any and every place, performing with cheerfulness the most unpleasant and disagreeable duties. The soldiers saw and felt that there was an interest in them. It did good to the men and women who work. We do not believe that any men or women who labored there regretted the labor or exposure. Many will consider it among the best spent days of their lives.

When we look at its strictly *religious character*, there is an interest which surmounts all others. There are thousands of men dying, who have only a few moments in which to make their preparations for eternity. Some of them ignorant of religious principles, others who have lived in ungodliness rejecting the offers of the Gospel when in health, others who have been hardened in their sins, and bold in their defiant contempt of religion and every thing connected with it. Here they are anxious for a word to be spoken to them about the Saviour, to have a portion of the Bible read, a prayer offered, a message sent to their parents. Others having lived in the hope of eternal life, are now waiting for the few moments to pass when they will enter on that rest.—They have words of comfort, messages of kindness and love which they want sent to their friends. They die among strangers, scattered in every direction; chaplains cannot reach the one-hundredth of them.

There are wounded who are in hope of living, but whom the Surgeon knows will die. Others are anxious and all through the thousands who on the battlefield have been made to realize the Scripture, that "there is but a step between me and death:" there is a readiness to hear and an anxiety to be spoken to about their souls, to hear the Gospel and the prayer of the Christian who will commend him to God. The loud and solemn call of God's Providence in their wounds, the fact of their escape from death, the vows which they made upon the field when wounded—everything tends to make them susceptible of receiving the word of life. Many cases of exceeding great interest are scattered over every field and every hospital, but scarcely a man can be found who does not give respectful attention.

The Commission not only sends her men to speak to them, but furnishes paper, ink, pens, &c. and men *to write the letters* which may be desired, and as an evidence of the extent to which this is carried on, we would remark that coming from the hospitals on the 7th or 8th of July, so soon after the battle, we brought a pair of saddle-bags containing over 500 letters, to the Baltimore post-office, which bore glad as well as sad tidings to at least that many hundred families.

As soon as the men are so composed that they can read; tracts, religious papers, and books are furnished, with copies of the New Testament. It would surprise any one who had not mingled among these scenes to learn the demand for the Scriptures, and the amount of religious reading of every kind put into circulation and read with attention and interest by the men. We doubt much, whether among the same number of persons in any part of our Christian communities, there could be found as many careful and attentive readers and hearers of Gospel truths as in the field encompassed by these hospitals. Men who lost their Testaments in the battle, anxiously inquired for a copy. Not a case, as far as could be found, would go unsupplied.

It is one of the great fields which God has opened to bring the truth of His word to the hearts of the very class of our youth, who, in peace and prosperity at home, are wont to turn a deaf ear. We doubt not but that God will bring more trophies to the Gospel of His Son from these wounded than from the same number of young men who are daily hearing its invitations. We look upon the instrumentality which God has raised up in this Commission as admirably suited to their wants. It comes without *the formality* of the church, and the organ and the pulpit, and the set discourses, the round of etiquette and mannerism, which keeps the common people at a respectful distance. It approaches right up to a man, and, without any ceremony, tries to meet his case; it makes a man lying in a cow stall, a barn-yard, a shed, under a tree, even in the mud, feel that "he is a man for a' that," and has a soul which must be saved by the blood of Jesus; must come to Him *there*, must trust Him *there*, must be saved *there*, or not be saved. What a degradation of the office of the ministry, some will think, for a minister of the Gospel preaching in a cowstable, under a straw and cattle-shed, in the entry of a barn, on the loose boards, over a stable when the straw had been removed to make bedding for those on the ground. If this wants dignity—is out of place—is unbecoming a minister, then the Master did not set us a proper example, who was himself born in a manger, and preached to helpless, diseased, & &c. If the object is to reach such as he reached and preach the Gospel to such as he preached it to, we must go to these very places and persons. Hence the propriety of the name *Christian Commission*. Men in these very places want to hear of Jesus, be prayed with and pointed to the kingdom of heaven. Many interesting cases occur daily that might fill a whole report.

It has been a source of great gratification to meet men among these wounded as we have passed, calling us by name, and reminding us that we preached to their regiment at such a place; another to their company at such a bridge, in such a barrack, or along the railroad track, &c. It has satisfied us, if we had any doubt before, that these men, who appear careless in the company of their companions, do yet regard the Gospel when preached to them; and we would here say also, that from the time when we preached to the 1st *Maryland*, under *Colonel Kenly*, at Camp Carroll, to the last time, in a tent at Gettysburg General Hospital, we have invariably had the most respectful attention.

At Shriver's barn, a lad 21 years of age was pointed out by the surgeon as one who could not live but a day or so. After conversing and praying with him, we wrote for him—"Remember me to all at home; I hope to see the little ones." Such was the condition of filth that we had to stand on a rail.

In a barn near Hunterstown road lay a young lad, an orphan, on the bare floor wounded in the side and breast, just ready to die; we roused him up after several attempts, learned his name and home. Pointing him to Jesus, quoted that text: "Him that cometh unto me I will in no wise cast out." With an effort he said: "*I have been thinking a good deal about that text.*" In half an hour he was dead.

Four miles out on the Chambersburg road, as we came among some tents on the south side of the road, one of the surgeons asked if we were a minister, that there was one of the men who would soon die. He could not eat anything. We had a few oranges, one of which we parted into one of the small divisions, and the first time we noticed his mouth open, put it in, so that in closing his lips he would taste it. As he drew them together, without any knowledge of whence it came from, he said: "*That don't taste bad.*" So gradually we succeeded in getting him to take nearly, if not half, an orange. By this time he was so much refreshed that he could talk. He was wounded in breast and right shoulder. After talking to and praying with him, he desired us to write to "his father and mother, to try to meet him in God, in peace." Several other cases in the same tents might be repeated. He died in a day or two.

At the Court House were some interesting cases, As we passed up a young man from Luzerne Co., Pa., who had come over to take home his brother, asked us to go and pray with him, for he was afraid he would not live to get home. "He had left a comfortable home to go and fight for his country" was his tender and brotherly remark. We found him in the corner of the Catholic church, but on seeing him, knew that his days were numbered. We conversed and prayed with him. In a few days we aided in getting his body home.

A view of the battlefield early on Monday, July 6th, was anything but pleasant. In every direction were dead horses, which from the heat were as offensive as they could be. Here and there were bodies of men unburied, and at other places were men just dying, with no person near to do anything for them. As we passed from a little house between the Taneytown and Emmittsburg road, adjoining a little orchard and near Gen. Meade's headquarters, which had been riddled with shot and shell, we noticed one on the ground dead, another on the floor of an old stable or little barn dying; but we could do nothing for him. He was past all help. We could not learn anything of either of them. Beside, there were so many thousands to whom service might be rendered, that we felt it a duty to leave these to the men who were appointed to see after them. That afternoon or next day we found three or four men engaged in burying them.

The appearance of the field was as if an army of men, with every kind of material, had started up in the night, leaving everything but what was fastened to their bodies. Knapsacks, blankets, coats, hats, shoes, stockings, testaments, letters, cards, plates, knives, bread, crackers, meat, candles, cartridge boxes, percussion caps, and bullets without count, ramrods drawn to load, and in the fury of battle thrown away to use their bayonet or butt of the gun, broken guns, broken wagons of ammunition and of cannons, wheels that had been driven a hundred yards from the wagon by a cannon hall or shell, shells by the wagon load which had not yet exploded, solid shot, and fragments of shells in every direction.

The breastworks which our men had put upon the left of the Cemetery and on down toward round top, were line upon or back of lines, zig-zag, and curved according to the piece of ground and position.–They were made in places from the stone fences which ran nearly all around our lines; in other places, rails were built up, and earth dug up against them; also, in some places, against the walls. Destruction of fences was marked from below the round top, where Kilpatrick's cavalry had position along both sides of Taneytown, Emmittsburg, Baltimore and other roads. Fences were removed everywhere, for fortification, or fires as they needed.

The land seems to have no subsoil, and when it becomes wet, is miry, making it laborious if not dangerous traveling over it after rains. There was no fence left which made the least obstruction, from the hill back of the Seminary, across through the line where Hancock and Sedgwick's corps were, or Gen. Meade's headquarters, down through the 11th and 12th corps hospitals, to where we struck Rock Creek at the 2d corps hospital. The other corps hospitals were in the same vicinity. The 3d corps had a barn and house and tents of rebels. Their hospitals were on the west, north and north-east, under the names of the division commanders.

At the extreme right of Lee's army, they erected heavy breastworks, from Marsh Creek to their lines, to prevent our men from flanking them. East of this and south of where our 3d corps was on the second day, and in the neighborhood of which our men retreated when driven from the peach orchard, on the Emmittsburg road, to the round top, are a mass of *large rocks*, of very singular formation in a hollow, through which Plum run passes. This stream runs among and through these rocks. Between them are crevices of 10 to 15 deep, and about 1 1/2 to 2 feet wide. In the pursuit of our men, many of their men were wounded and killed on these rocks, who fell into the crevices, from which, if wounded, they could not well escape, and if killed, it would be with difficulty they could be found, and almost impossible to get them out. This whole neighborhood was rocky. When burying the many that were slain here, it was difficult to get earth to bury them, and in a few places, they had to be covered over with stone. In the latter part of August and first of September, when passing over this ground, in company with Rev. Dr. Junkin, we found some or these men still unburied. It is generally supposed that these were all Rebels; but in several cases we found the bodies wrapped in the overcoat of our men. In some of the hospitals we found some of our men who had been wounded there.

Death makes no distinction. There is no discharge in the war with death and the grave. The bullet, cannon ball or shell regards not the person in rank or position, or to what army; yet it is gratifying to see the respect shown, when opportunity is had, in the burying of individuals in spots, under trees, by a rock, near a stream, places where they call be found, with the inscription on a board, or cut in a tree, or on a rock. Under a pear tree, near a house, a short distance north of 11th corps hospital, on east side of Taneytown road, are buried side by side Lieutenant E. G. Grannis of Macon, Ga., and Col. James Huston of 2d N.Y. State Militia; both killed July 2d. These graves are neatly prepared. In a field between Rock Creek and turnpike, toward the 6th Corps Reserves, is buried Nelson A. Thayer, Company C, 123d New York Volunteers; below the rocks, in the lower part of a meadow, on the other side, also alone, is Marshal Prue, Company F, 5th Texas. A piece of rail, in each case, is driven in at the head of the grave, and the name written with a lead pencil.

We had daily cases calling upon us to aid in securing the passage of the body of a father, son, brother or husband. Mothers, wives and sisters from Wisconsin or Maine and all intermediate places to nurse their sons, and husbands and brothers, and fathers and brothers, would be found waiting upon their wounded and dying. A wife came to see and attend upon her wounded husband. She learned he was dead. She then desired to know where he was buried. Her informant said it was impossible to find him, remarking, "You might as well expect to find a needle in a hay-stack." "Is it as likely?" she said. He said, "just as likely." "Then," said she, "I can find him, for I could take apart every blade of hay until I had removed it entirely. Show me where he was buried?" She got help to go with her, and after disinterring some 12 to 22, as they had nearly uncovered the next body, she espied something by which she knew him, and jumping down into the grave, with her own hand scratched off the earth that covered his arm and aided in getting him out, and thus bore home with her the object of affection. What will not energy and perseverance, with heart and soul, interested, accomplish? The State of Pennsylvania, through her agent, afforded every facility in passing bodies over her railroads.

Every case in which we wrote for any one, it was the invariable request: "Give my love to the children, or my wife, or parents, and a hope to see them at home or meet them in heaven."

The Christian Commission at Gettysburg, though with some friction, *was one of the greatest successes,* evidencing all adaptedness which has never been excelled in the working of any benevolent, humane, and Christian enterprise. It could not be supposed that 400 men and women should come together in haste, many of whom had never seen each other before, of all classes—that they should all fall in and work together without any jealousy or collision. Some thought they went only to help wounded off the field of battle, and when that was done, there was nothing more for them; others only to help the surgeons. Some came because they had friends there. Some to attend to the wounded from their neighborhood. They would wish to be sent to that field in which they were. Mostly they said, "send us wherever we are most needed," and this was the general request. It is true, some came to seek out friends among the Rebel wounded. Some brought clothes, and others had them sent to them.

That it was the right and duty of the Government to forbid anything which would interfere with their plans is unquestionable. So in the hurry of the occasion, some came as delegates of the Commission, who ought not to have been there, and some professing to be, who were not commissioned. There were dozens of persons whom we never saw, and concerning whom we had neither time or opportunity to inquire. The work which for a week or two pressed itself, required every exertion which could be given. This we can say on the whole, that a more loyal, diligent, faithful, persevering company of men and women could not be gathered from any part of the Union.

When we started to go to the battlefield, it was to attend to our own wounded; we did not expect to have anything to do with the Rebel wounded. The object and origin of this Commission operation in the city of Baltimore, shortly after the 19th of April, 1861, was mainly to attend to our own soldiers first passing; then when sick and wounded; then when in the hospitals. Have we not been devoted to them in camps, barracks, hospitals ever since? With the same intent we made our way to the field at Gettysburg. As we attended our own men, beside them lay in alternate rows, and mixed through other, so that in mud, and dirt, and blood, and rags, and nakedness, with bodies wounded and torn in almost every way, but perfectly helpless, you could not distinguish unless they would speak, which were the Rebels. What would be expected of us at such a time, and under such circumstances?–When this rebellion was making its first moves to defeat the Government in getting its army, we heard a lady, who seemed to sympathize with the rebellion, propose to throw hot water on our soldiers as they passed. "You had better give them some bread and meat," said her husband. Finding these thousands of cases of wretched suffering men in our hands and in our power, would any one have us scald them to death? or let them die for want of care? or as the Samaritan, bind up their wounds, pour in on and wine, and take care of them?–(Luke, x: 33-37.)

We thought our loyalty which had gone through the days of April 19, 1861, which had face to face resisted every attempt at carrying out our own State, and battled until the enemy's power was broken in our midst, was sufficiently decided to venture on the principle and duty of feeding and caring for the bodies and souls of these men. Hence, when we had arranged in regard to our own and had hundreds at work for them, we felt it a duty to give special attention to look into the condition of those who lay in barns. sheds, stalls, pens, under trees, in tents, &c. 1. Humanity would have revolted at us if we had not done it. 2. Christianity demanded it as a duty. 3. The honor of our country required it. These men were in our hands, and our Government was responsible before God and the whole world to take care of them. If the rebel Government can afford to treat wounded men unkindly, we cannot. 4. It was only good policy. Will not these men, and will not the Rebels be bound to treat our men better? Several of their surgeons remarked to us: "If any of your men should ever get down among us as we are with you, we can't do for you as you have done for us, *but we will do the very best we can.*" 5. If the Government is to be successful in putting down this rebellion, which we never for one moment doubted, will it not help to bring us together in kindlier relations, to feel that while in war and battle they will be met and treated as men, enemies with all the power of the nation, yet when wounded and helpless, and are brought into our hospitals, they shall be carefully and faithfully attended to? A man gained by proper attention is as good as one gained by a bullet. 6. Many of them are as decided Union men, if they dare be, as some of our own, and much more so than the Copperheads that have come to our notice. Over and over again have we heard men from Mississippi, Alabama and North Carolina say of their own accord: "If we had this matter in our hands we could settle it in five minutes;" "that they never wanted any better Government than they had; never expected as good a one again." As we passed among the Rebels at the 3d corps one day, in company with Mr. Frances, ex-President of the Pennsylvania Senate, a man from North Carolina said he hoped the Government would not stop until they brought every — one of them into the Union. At this same hospital was a nephew of Andrew Johnson, from Tennessee, who, with ninety-four other young men, in 1862, started for Kentucky, to enter the Union cavalry. On September 10 they were captured near Luckey Cove Seminary, Powell Valley, Lee Co., Va. Since then most of them were killed and taken prisoners. He was sent to Staunton, and put in the 8th Virginia infantry, and had been in service until wounded here. He and his friends were strong Union men. He not only gave evidence of his faith and hope in Christ, but expressed the joy which it would have given him if he could have fallen in the defence of his country, which he desired to serve. 7. From all experience of over eight weeks, we are perfectly satisfied that if the war was ended tomorrow, and their rulers, leaders and politicians were out of the way, there would be the kindest feeling, commingling together with sorrow over the bereavements, and that the men of both sides would mourn together over the evils which have fallen upon both. The cry that we must separate because we can't live together is perfectly absurd, being mere slang to keep up the rebellion.

8. Above all, *let us do right*; as Henry Clay, that noble patriot and statesman, said, "*I'd rather be right than be President.*"

We avoided political discussion with the Rebels, on the ground that it is ungenerous to strike a wounded man who is in your power, and all impropriety unbecoming the object which we had in view, which was to minister to their bodies and their souls. But on several occasions when the subject was introduced, we remarked, this war was to accomplish God's purpose. God had His own design in it, which He would make manifest in due time but it would not probably be what either part aimed at. We had gotten rich, proud and corrupt; we had encouraged politicians until they had become so corrupt, it was almost a necessity that there should be a breaking down of Government to destroy their power: that the young had taken control of their parents, defying law and order, and making rebellion against God and the laws of the nation honorable. "That is just the way my father talked and preached before I came away," said a young man from Mississippi, who was badly wounded, and lying on a bed in the tent, with but little prospect of living.

We met wounded North Carolinians in almost every direction. At one place, as we required of some wounded men from whence they were, "North Carolina" was the answer. "How is it that we find North Carolina almost everywhere?" "The only reason we can give for it," answered a young man, "is that they try to wreak *their vengeance* upon us because our State was opposed to going out of the Union. They put us in every dangerous and exposed place, and give us the hard end of everything." Another said, "My part of the State was opposed to going out, and they brought all army in on us, and compelled us to go with them."

In looking at this battle and the circumstances surrounding it, we were deeply impressed with the conviction that the whole of this battle was of God; that His controlling providence had, in a most marked manner, evidenced itself in the time, place, arrangements and success. Any one who will read Gen. Lee's account of his advance into Pennsylvania and down to Gettysburg, the battle of the 1st and 2d days, will see that he did not expect to meet Gen. Meade there, nor could have wanted it there, nor could Gen. Meade, in the haste with which he had to meet him, have designed it there; yet every rock and hill seemed to have been prepared for it.

We are no less impressed with the truth, that war is a most fearful judgment of God upon a nation and people. This is a national judgment. God is punishing North and South, East and West. Before it is over, not less than one million of the young men, the flower and hope of the country, will have slept in the earth, buried without honor or distinction; the pride of man laid in the very lowest place; contempt thrown by God upon all the boasting and glorying of man. But God's work will be done. The nation will be humbled. Lamentation and mourning will go into almost every family. The pride of the oppressor will be broken. "The loftiness of man shall be bowed down, the haughtiness of men shall be made low, and the Lord alone shall be exalted."–Isaiah ii: 11-17.

Nothing so effectually depletes a nation of its overgrown wealth and strength as war. Like the bleeding and blistering of the body to reduce it, so God applies the judgment which will effect his end. Every battle has a great purpose to perform. Not what man aims at; but what God has designed. How remarkable are the facts connected with the greatest battles ever fought! A shower of rain defeated Napoleon at Waterloo, retarding his operations. A mist intervened between the ships of Nelson, which would have seized him when returning from Egypt to France, and enabled him to escape. The miscalculation of time, the range of a gun, the construction of a shell, the cutting of a telegraph wire, the burning of a bridge, the change of commanders, the coming up of reinforcements, all the work, apparently, of a moment, producing a necessity, showing that God can lay aside any man, foil any plan, blow upon any army.

God's judgments do not cease until He effects His end. If war does not do it, famine and pestilence will. His purposes ripen fast in time of war. They are the great political throes through which He produces such changes in the face of the political world as bring on the state of things which shall prepare the way for the coming of the kingdom of His Son. This very war has done more to make the people of this nation know one another, than all the histories published since we were a nation. Hundreds of thousands, north and south, have changed their places and positions. They have been brought face to face, to see and feel that they are the same men. They converse in the field, in the interim of battle; they lie together in the same hospital and tent; they talk and feel together, so that the very means which were designed of the leaders to produce permanent disunion, brings them together, and makes them feel that they are one people.

The history of this rebellion will show a despotism in the Rebel leaders which has seldom happened in the world. "Their violent dealings will come down upon their own pates." Psalms vii: 6. No man could go through the Rebel hospitals, and see the fearful slaughter which was made among their wounded men, without feeling, as Gen. Lee says, "More may have been required of them than they were able to perform," or, as many of them said, "We were driven up into *slaughter pens*." A day of reckoning will come.

The sight of the wounded, dying and dead is surely enough to convince any one that war is most horrible, conducted on the best principles, and can be accounted for only on the principle that it is one of God's "four score judgments" which he visits upon nations for their wickedness.–Ezekiel xiv: 21.

It may appear singular that in the advance of the Gospel, so fearful a struggle should take place in a Christian nation, just following one of the most remarkable periods of prayer ever known in the history of the world. We must, however, remember that God's way is in the storm and whirlwind.–Nahum i: 3; that he maketh the clouds his chariots, and walketh upon the wings of the wind.–Psalms civ: 3. Political revolutions and civil wars break down and root out national evils. As we advance to the fulfilling of the seventh angel's trumpet, we must look for revolutions greater than have ever been since the foundation of the earth–(Rev. xvi: 17-21.)

We must not forget for a moment that God sitteth upon the whirlwind and directs the storm to do His own sovereign purposes. So change can take place which shall hinder the coming of the kingdom of His Son. All the overturnings in the earth are to prepare the way for His coming.–Ezekiel xxi: 27. Christians may confidently trust their Lord and master who is at the helm of the vessel, as well as he who holds the winds in his fist.–Prov. vi: 20. He will make all things to work for their individual good, and the general welfare of his cause. The probability is, that the soldiers who come out of the armies will be as active and devoted Christians as could be found among the same number of men anywhere on the earth. Every revolution in the earth is to break down some institution of Satan. He will rave and storm and threaten. His agents and even good men, bewildered and controlled by him as an angel of light, will see nothing but destruction.

Two years since, we heard a minister of the Gospel say "*the grave was dug and the coffin being made ready for the burial of this nation,*" which God gave to our fathers. When *Wickcliffe*, the morning star of the Reformation, was dangerously ill, the mendicant friars sent deputies to induce him before he died, to revoke what he had said against them. Recovering his spirits and raising himself on his pillow he said, "*I shall not die, but live to declare the evil deeds of the friars.*" Our country did not die in 1861, was not buried, the grave was not dug, the coffin was not prepared, though we were invited to the funeral. Like that morning star she has risen higher and shines brighter. The clouds are dispersing; soon the daylight will shine so clear that we may see her condition and when the sun appears will know indeed that the night of her tribulation but preceded a brighter day.

We could not then and do not now believe that God was going to destroy so many Christian people for the wickedness of the unprincipled politicians who had been and were seeking to govern or destroy this nation. Wicked rebellion did almost overthrow David's throne; but God delivered him. Multitudes of lives were sacrificed on both sides; but God overthrew the rebellion. When men say that the Union cannot be established, they forget, that after all, truth and righteousness are stronger than all evil; that God is stronger than Satan and will make the wrath of man and malice of hell to praise Him in preparing the way for the coming of the kingdom of His Son. When the warfare of God's people was nearly accomplished, he commanded the prophet to comfort them and to call upon them "to prepare the way for His coming, assuring them that every valley should be exalted, every mountain and hill be made low and the crooked places made straight (Isaiah 40th ch.,) the rough places plain." Thus God, in His Providence, by the Whirlwind of passion among men and his stormy wind, fulfills His word.–Psalms cxlviii: 8. Those who may live will see that this storm and whirlwind through this nation, has prepared it for greater good to mail with greater glory to God than probably any revolt which has taken place the past three centuries!

We look upon the operations of this Christian Commission, prudently managed as one of the great *counter actants* to the suffering and wickedness which is a constant accompaniment of war and is an institution itself showing the advance of the Gospel against the power of the devil.

The enemy that fell into our hands received nothing more than it was our duty to render them as wounded. If nations at war will not attend to the wounded of their enemies in their hands, they are getting back into a barbarism with which Christianity can have no alliance.

The work of the Christian Commission after the battle at Gettysburg is an exhibition of what it has done and can do. Let no man or woman complain of labor, sacrifice or self-denial in the service rendered or contributions given. These men whom we sought to comfort were your fathers, husbands, brothers, and sons. They have given their time, strength, their limbs, and many, very many of them, their lives, that they might secure you in the enjoyment of the comforts and safety which are your inheritance. Do you grudge the help they received? or will you withhold help now when the demand comes from so many parts of the nation, and from so many of the wounded and, dying, who have given all and life too to protect you?

What are a few dollars, or a few pair of socks, shirts, drawers, pants, &c., or the bread, dried fruit, delicacies, &c., to the time the delegates of the Commission have given in attending upon the wounded? But what are any and all which do not involve life? *Life, life,* is what they give, who face the bullet and bayonet, and shot and shell, to guard your homes and save your country.

We would suggest that the operations of the Commission are too heavy, and require too much time, labor and attention to be continued on mere extempore agents. Men will on emergencies, as at Gettysburg, turn out for a few days, or a week or two, but there are labors to be performed for months after such a battle, and many of these call only be performed to advantage by experienced persons, who remain with them.

Ministers of Evangelical denominations, devoted and experienced, are needed in the service of the Commission. We disparage no man's field of labor when we say, that a minister who is adapted to the work cannot find a field where he may more immediately and directly preach the Gospel. While experienced men are needed, we believe it to be the grandest field for a young minister to learn pastoral theology. Highly as we appreciate instructions on the subject, we believe that the young ministers of our day, who will enter heart and soul in this work, will get more practical and useful pastoral training than from all books and lectures.

It is a marvelous thing that in these last days, two immense armies should have such extraordinary efforts made for their salvation by the people on both sides. Nor is it less wonderful that the Spirit of God has been so largely poured out on both armies. Such things have never taken place before, except in the days of Cromwell. God has some great and glorious end in view, which we do not yet see. Let us trust in Him, labor and wait, looking for the day of his appearing. "He will come to be glorified in His saints, and to be admired in all them that believe." ✥

John Calhoun Chamberlain
SPECIAL COLLECTIONS, BOWDOIN COLLEGE

A Delegate's Diary

✛ ✛ ✛ ✛ ✛ ✛ ✛

John Calhoun Chamberlain

THE FIRST CHRISTIAN COMMISSION delegates at Gettysburg, Rowland Howard and John C. Chamberlain, shared a common story. Both men graduated from Bowdoin College, and then attended Bangor Theological Seminary. They found themselves in the small Pennsylvania town while following units commanded by their brothers. Rowland's brother was the well-known General Oliver O. Howard, commander of the Eleventh Corps. John's brother, Lawrence, had recently been promoted to the colonelcy of the Twentieth Maine Regiment.

John Chamberlain's trip south had been germinating for several months. In February 1863, his younger brother, Lieutenant Thomas Chamberlain, wrote, "If I were you I would come out here next vacation for it would not cost more than sixteen doll's and I think we shall be here some two months yet." Following Lawrence's promotion on May 20, 1863, the brothers renewed their invitation. On May 22, the Colonel wrote, "We shall probably be situated for some little time so that you could find it pleasant to visit us. The season is glorious. Our camp is fine & you would thoroughly enjoy it. I shall be expecting you soon now."[1]

The warm entreaty convinced John to make the journey, leaving within days of its receipt. During a stop in Boston, he enrolled as a delegate of the

[1] Thomas Chamberlain to John C. Chamberlain, 2 February 1863, Special Collections, Fogler Library, University of Maine, Orono, Maine; JCC to Joshua Lawrence Chamberlain, 6 March 1863, Chamberlain-Adams Correspondence, Schlesinger Library, Radcliffe College, Harvard University, Cambridge, Massachusetts; JLC to JCC, 22 May 1863. Joshua L. Chamberlain Papers, Collections of the Manuscript Division, Library of Congress, Washington, D. C.

Rowland B. Howard
SPECIAL COLLECTIONS
BOWDOIN COLLEGE

United States Christian Commission, seizing the opportunity to give a
purpose for his trip while taking advantage of the free train passes given to
delegates. Chamberlain understood, however, that it was not a lark. As he
headed south, he stopped in Philadelphia to visit the national headquarters
of the Commission, meeting George H. Stuart, its chairman. Here, the
Commission issued the "standard" delegate kit: a haversack, a rubber ground
cloth, a tin cup, and a leather-bound journal. This volume included instructions for the delegates and blank pages for entries. As part of the superb
public relations work of the Commission, delegates shared the journals with
the central office, where poignant stories were transcribed and mailed to the
major Northern newspapers and periodicals.

The journal traces the Chamberlain's life over the next six weeks, as he
served along with some thirty-five other men at Christian Commission
stations in Virginia. When the camps broke, he finally caught up with his
brothers on June 22 near Aldie. Marching north with the Twentieth Maine,
John shared in the excitement of the unfolding events. He recalled the
morning of July 2, writing:

> As we advanced we saw nothing that told of the battle, except now and
> then, at long intervals, a dash of smoke from the heights held by Howard.

As we drew nearer, however, the hospitals told the story of what had been and what was to come. Our forces proceeded right up in line of battle, and speedily every hill was capped with smoke, the most terrific cannonading on right, on left and front—the whizzing and bursting of shells, and the clatter of musketry.[2]

Those bursting shells led the Colonel to issue a brotherly order: "Boys, I don't like this. Another such shot might make it hard for mother. Tom, go to the rear of the regiment, and see that it is well closed up! John, pass up ahead and look out for a place for our wounded." Two brothers rode off to the end of the Union line on Little Round Top. John proceeded to the rear, encountering the wounded on the way. He recalled,

...lying under every tree, the woods seemed full of them, they issued from every path and were scattered along the road-sides. They were wandering around searching for their respective hospitals. It was a very small portion who could be accommodated in ambulances. Many of their hospitals I was able to point out to them after washing their wounds. Poor fellows! after reaching their hospitals many of them were little better off. The houses and barns would hold but a handful.[3]

Watching the sun blaze down on the men, Chamberlain improvised makeshift shelters to cover their faces, using blankets, stones, and sticks.

For the next three days, John worked in hospitals behind the Union lines, watching each incoming stretcher and ambulance for a brother's face. Chaos left severe shortages of supplies and no regular means of distribution. Late on July 4, after learning of a nearby field hospital that lacked supplies and staff, Chamberlain set off into the dark, avoiding the carcasses and broken wagons that still blocked the roads. He found the Surgeon-in-charge sick with some two hundred wounded left in the care of his overwhelmed assistant. Hoping to find needed supplies, Chamberlain headed down the road to a reputed Sanitary Commission station, only to find nothing there.

[2] John C. Chamberlain to Charles Demond, 11 July 1863, newspaper clipping, Edward Tobey Papers, Massachusetts Historical Society, Boston, Massachusetts.

[3] John Pullen, *The Twentieth Maine: A Volunteer Regiment in the Civil War* (Philadelphia: 1957), 110.

It was late; he was very weary; it was nearly five miles to Gettysburg, where the station of the Christian Commission was, the road was hard, and the streams all high and swollen. But the men were suffering, and there was no one but him to help. He took the long and lonely walk, and very early the next morning the wagon of the Christian Commission was at that hospital, laden with stores and comforts.[4]

In his official report to the Christian Commission, he wrote:

This is the way I spent my time at Gettysburg—going round the hospitals, reading in the faces of the men their wants and trying to relieve them, speaking words of comfort and religious consolation, and gathering their dying messages to their friends at home.... There are a thousand little nameless acts, which the world cannot know, nor we ourselves recall, that are nonetheless important in their issues. The grateful soldier notes them, one by one, and thanks God for the Christian Commission.[5]

Chamberlain did not see his brothers again until July 5 as he entered the regiment's camp. "If I ever shook hands heartily," John recalled, "I did so then, as I looked on Lawrence and Thomas alive." He decided to go south with the Twentieth Maine rather than stay at Gettysburg. As they marched out of town, the Colonel pointed out Little Round Top to his brother.

The next two weeks proved eventful. The hard marching and poor weather caught up with him and he fell ill. After recovering for five days in the house of a Maryland minister, John took a circuitous route to Washington, ending up in a jail cell near Relay House just outside of Baltimore. Under orders to watch closely for spies and deserters, Union troops detained him overnight. Chamberlain's account of his captivity is bitter—he had proper credentials—and yet full of wit, even as they marched him through town at bayonet point.

Upon reaching the capital, Chamberlain resigned his delegate's commission and returned to home and studies. The following summer, he received his degree from Bangor Theological Seminary. He traveled south

[4] Edward P. Smith, *Incidents of the Christian Commission* (Philadelphia: J. B. Lippincott, 1868), 161-162.

[5] John C. Chamberlain to Charles Demond, 11 July 1863, newspaper clipping, Edward Tobey Papers, Massachusetts Historical Society, Boston, Massachusetts.

again in August 1864, visiting his older brother as he lay close to death in an Annapolis hospital. When Lawrence came home to recover in late September, the Colonel showed his support for the Christian Commission by attending a local fund-raising meeting.[6]

His studies complete, Chamberlain moved to New York City, preaching twice a week until he found a position as a clerk in the Department of Internal Revenue. After Tom resigned from the army, he came to live nearby, working for a time in his brother's office. This happy domestic scene was complete when John married Delia Jarvis of Castine, Maine, in September 1866.[7]

For all his apparent good fortune, a dark cloud of illness hung over Chamberlain. He never fully recovered from a bout with tuberculosis in 1859, a condition that undoubtedly prevented him from enlisting in the army with his brothers. The disease returned in the spring of 1865. By April 1867, with his health deteriorating rapidly, John moved to Castine, where he spent his last months as a minister and teacher. Following his death on August 10, he was buried in Brewer, Maine. His family believed that his service with the Christian Commission contributed to his early demise.[8]

The document that follows is a transcription of John Chamberlain's Christian Commission journal with editor's additions placed within brackets. He made his first entries shortly after he received the diary in Philadelphia, and made regular entries until Sunday, June 21, when he left the volume in Washington, D. C. In mid-July, he completed the journal with a summary of the events surrounding the battle of Gettysburg and his return trip to the nation's capital. If John had not been the brother of the "hero of Little Round Top," this diary would still be significant for its description of the earliest work of the Christian Commission at Gettysburg.

In the late summer of 1986 family members found the diary at the summer cottage of Joshua Chamberlain's granddaughter Rosamond Allen. It is now in the collection of the Pejepscot Historical Society in Brunswick, Maine. ✢

---

[6] John C. Chamberlain to Gen. John L. Hodsdon, 22 July 1864, Maine State Archives; Alice Rains Trulock, *In the Hands of Providence: Joshua L. Chamberlain and the American Civil War* (Chapel Hill: University of North Carolina Press, 1992), 219.

[7] Diana Halderman Loski, *The Chamberlains of Brewer* (Gettysburg: Thomas Publications, 1998), 76-80.

[8] Trulock, 512.

✛   ✛   ✛

LEFT HOME JUNE 1st, 1863 to accept the urgent invitation of the Col. & Adjt. of the 20th Maine Regt.[1] and make them a visit. I [am] to go to Stoneman's Station and they on their part to meet me there with a grey horse saddled and ready to escort their brother and guest two miles to their camp. Sarah[2] debated a long time the propriety of accepting his invitation to accompany me and wisely gave it up.

At Boston I stopped at Parker's and saw the metropolis after a 3 years absence from it. Saw all the improvements, visited the new attractions, Bierstadt's Rocky Mountains and Sunday among the Pilgrims.[3] C. Davis of College acquaintance was polite to me. Visited Aunt Susan and concluded to see the Agent of Christian Commission, Mr. Demond.[4] He encouraged me to go on the service of the Commission and see my brothers at the same time, thought it my duty to do so. A letter from Uncle Sweet and he made out my papers and gave me $20 the same afternoon.

3rd, I left for Washington. Stopped only at Philadelphia (at Stuarts).[5] Putting up at the Continental Hotel. Went to Fairmount Park and water works and still insist that it is the most picturesque scenery (and well adorned by art too) I have ever seen. Other people don't see it so. I do. Independence Hall, etc., I saw. I could not get lost in Philadelphia if I should try to. The regularity of the city, so different from Northern cities, charmed me.

At 12, June 4, I left and the next day early found myself at my destination, the city of magnificent distances, the glorious national metropolis Washington. It was the 6th or 7th before we left it. We had time to visit the Capitol and White House and all the public buildings, Smithsonian, Patent Office where all Washington's Mt. Vernon relicts had been transported, etc. Mr. Small

[1] His brothers, Colonel Joshua Chamberlain and Adjutant Thomas Chamberlain.

[2] His sister, Sarah Chamberlain.

[3] Artist Albert Bierstadt (1830-1902) created a popular sensation in 1863 when he placed his massive painting, "The Rocky Mountains, Lander's Peak," on display at the Boston Atheneum.

[4] Charles Demond was the Secretary of the Boston Christian Commission and an original member of the United States Christian Commission board.

[5] George Stuart, the Chairman of the United States Christian Commission, maintained the organization's headquarters in his Philadelphia warehouse at 11 Bank Street.

accompanied me, was agreeable, free and companionable.[6] The Capitol was grand, the Prest's mansion disappointed us, ordinary city merchants have more neat and tasteful, if not more princely habitations. The back premises were very much neglected, glass broken out, fences propped up, paint worn off, weeds flourishing, walks not trim and tidy, the whole garden was very ordinary, lacked care and taste.

Saturday June 6th, 1863.

After wearisome delays we succeeded in getting on board the Steamer Lady Lincoln and glided down by Washington's residence and innumerable forts and reached Acquia Creek. Saw Marden[7] and dined on the queerest dinner I ever saw. Reached Falmouth in afternoon and after viewing city and getting caught in a shower with Small, returned to a beautiful supper. In the evening went to Lacy House[8] prayer meeting and exhorted. Here I am on the Potomac and Rappahannock and no white horse all saddled up and waiting at Stonemans. 5th Corps up river!

Sunday 7th.

Went up opposite Fredericks[burg] in morning and followed down the path of pickets on rivers edge to pontoon bridges. Came to Lacy House to morning service at 10 1/2. Prof. Day[9] of Lane Seminary Cin[cinnati] conducted service and Rev. Dr. Hall[10] of Trenton, N. J., made remarks. I closed with prayer. Then met Caldwell and with his glass examined the tomb of Washington's mother and three Rebel pickets. Lunched on bread as soft as crackers and jelly, apple butter, peaches preserved, pickled apples, onions, etc. Messrs. Small and Ewing[11] went horseback. In afternoon attended Mrs. Harris' Bible class.[12]

[6] Reverend A. K. P. Small, of Bangor, Maine, was a USCC delegate.

[7] George Marden graduated from Bangor Theological Seminary in 1862 and became pastor of the Boxborough, Massachusetts, Congregational Church in October 1863.

[8] Lacy House was a large house across the Rappahannock River from Fredericksburg.

[9] George Day was professor of theology at Lane Theological Seminary in Cincinnati.

[10] John Hall was pastor of the First Presbyterian Church of Trenton.

[11] Possibly Thompson Ewing of Pittsburgh, Pennsylvania.

[12] Mrs. Ellen Orbison Harris of Philadelphia was secretary of the Philadelphia Ladies' Aid Society throughout the war. Christian Commission publications regularly cited her work as an extension of its own.

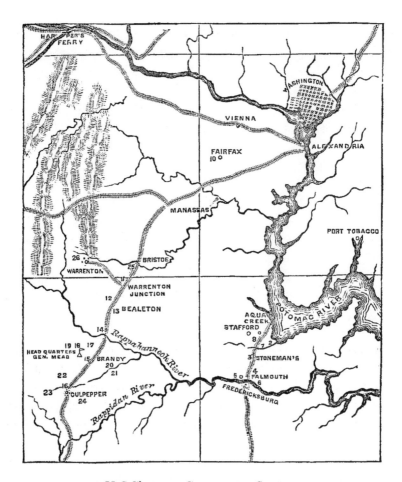

U. S Christian Commission Stations

1. Acquia Creek Station.	14. Rappahannock Station.
2. Belle Plain & Windmill Point.	15. Brandy Station.
3. Stoneman's Station.	16. Culpeper Station.
4. Falmouth Station.	17. River Station.
5. Falmouth Village Station.	18. Artillery Reserve, 2.
6. White Oak Station.	19. Artillery Station.
7. Potomac Creek Station.	20. Mountain Run Station.
8. Howard Station.	21. Cole Hill Station.
9. Brooks' Station.	22. Bullock Station.
10. Fairfax Station.	23. Sperryville Pike Station.
11. Warrenton Junction Station.	24. Pine Hill Station.
12. Germantown Station.	25. Briscoe Station.
13. Bealeton Station.	26. Warrenton City Station.

In the evening the communion administered by Prof. Day and Rev. Dr. Hall. Very (imposing) impressive. On way to tent, called into a Negro slave, genuine howler, faces up, elbows wriggling and swinging their bodies. One would sing one line, then, chorus of all "For there's always shouting in Heaven." It seemed to be a narrative mixed up of all the striking historic facts in the Old Testament and New. Slept with Prof. Day and rather coldly.

Monday 8th, 1863.
In the morning went up to the ruins of the Phillips mansion,[13] looked like the picture of English castle. At 11 came to Stoneman's Switch and sent a letter to the Col. by supply train. Fell in with two polite chaps from Commission who were in the same foolish predicament I was, looking for 5th Corps. Then came down to Acquia Creek and got lemons and papers of Marden to distribute among the soldiers of the Cavalry Corps on the hill. One tent never heard preaching since coming and had no Bibles.

Tuesday 9th.
At Acquia Creek with Day and Marden till evening came, then, got on cars for Potomac Creek. On way met Henry Farrar[14] right from Richmond prison. He is on Gen'l. Sedgwick's Staff with Tommy Hyde.[15] Arrived in the heat and found Henry solemnly at dinner, soon woke him up. In P.M. was introduced to the "Angel" Mrs. McKay and discovered Charlotte Johnson.[16] Took her

[13] Phillips House, across the Rappahannock River from Fredericksburg, served as General Ambrose Burnside's headquarters during the battle in December 1862.

[14] Henry W. Farrar of Bangor, Maine, mustered out of the army on 1 August 1865.

[15] Thomas Worcester Hyde of Bath, Maine, graduated from Bowdoin College in 1861. He raised a company for the Seventh Maine Infantry, then was elected major. He was with General Sedgwick at Gettysburg. He was promoted to lieutenant colonel, and later commissioned colonel of the First Maine Veteran Volunteers, ending his military career as a brigadier general. In 1873, Hyde was elected to the state senate, where he served three terms, two as president of that body. He was founder and president of Bath Iron Works.

[16] Charlotte Johnson McKay was a widow from Reading, Massachusetts, who volunteered as a nurse, working primarily with the Seventeenth Maine Regiment in which her brother served. Chamberlain expected to meet the well-known "Angel" and was surprised that he knew her already from her years in Brewer, Maine.

ambulance for Howard's Hdqtrs. Saw Charly and the Gen'l.[17] Rode horseback and saw Brigade drill—all the maneuvers of battle. In evening took charge of prayer meeting at Potomac Creek. After meeting fell in with a hard case. It was a man from the 6th Corps Hospital by the name of D. E. Boyden[18] of Duxbury, Vt. who left Middlebury College in 2nd year and enlisted as private in the first 3 months Regiment that left Vermont. Two days, or next day after his first battle, Big Bethel, he was taken sick from exhaustion and placed unconscious in the hospital with Typhoid fever. He partially recovered so as to be able to accompany the Regiment home but had a severe relapse before he reached home and the surgeon telegraphed his parents to come and see him die. Before he was able to shoulder a musket he enlisted in the 6th Vt. for the war, as 2nd Sergeant. Soon he was promoted to Sergeant Major. At White Oak Swamp he was shot in head, back, and hip, examined and left on the field for dead. He was a prisoner a month and his position was filled by another when he was released, so he was obliged to return to 2nd Sergeant. At Antietam was again wounded for life in hip and being 8 months in the hospital, came out a private. He joined the Regiment Sunday evening at midnight and the next morning at 6 was in the charge of Fredericksburg and before sunset was shot through the side. The ball passing between his ribs, cutting out a piece of his lung, and coming out near the spine as I saw by his coat, and here again he was left on the field speechless and losing blood. A hail storm and rain set in and there he lay 4 days. In the meantime he had lost 2 brothers, an uncle, 3 cousins and 3 more wounded. He was in Big Bethel, Yorktown Siege, Williamsburg, Richmond Siege and 7 days fight, saw 5 days fighting at South Mountain, Sharpsburg and Fredericksburg 2nd. Twice his effects were sent home and his family in mourning for weeks. He had read his own obituary and this I call a hard case. He is still cheerful and trusts in the Lord, calmly waiting. It was in the prayer meeting I met him and learned his history. Afterwards he repeated it for me to note down. But he calls himself lucky—his case is one of a thousand right around the camps here. O! the unspeakable suffering of war.

[17] The "Gen'l" refers to General Oliver O. Howard, a graduate of Bowdoin College. "Charly," his brother, Charles Henry Howard (Bowdoin 1859) was a Bvt. Brigadier General who saw action at Bull Run, Antietam, Fredericksburg, Gettysburg and Chattanooga, and in command of the U. S. C. T. training camp at Beaufort, S. C.

[18] Dexter E. Boyden was discharged on 2 November 1864.

Wednesday [10th].

In morning went out with oranges, lemons, and Silent Comforters[19] among the soldiers of 3rd Corps, 3rd Division. In the afternoon arranged and numbered 150 books in the library. Went out to the hospital graveyard, etc. In the evening we had a howler. Such earnestness and grappling on G[od] in prayer. I never joined in the most methodistical revival. It was very commendable. In these circumstances who would not shout. The tent was jambed. The poor sick fellows sitting on poles for our planks have not come.[20]

Thursday 11th.

In the morning [went] on the field alloted to me, 6th Corps, 1st Division and distributed a basket of papers, lemons, etc. Found many Maine boys who were glad to see me. In P.M. called on Mrs. McKay and she gave me her ambulance and I visited the 3rd Corps which had just struck tent and I saw 15,000 men with all the circumstances of war, knapsack and all accoutrements on their back and a loaf of bread on their bayonets (for they charged on their bakery as they passed by) pass by me face to face and wind among the valleys so the Rebels couldn't see them with their glasses. The Zouaves were conspicuous. Tonight they say the whole army is moving and tomorrow I expect the boom and thunder of artillery will awake my "peaceful slumbering" on a board. In the afternoon, last part, I went to the 5th Corps Hospital where the 20th Maine men complained of hard usage and hard officers, but [they] said better times are now for we have as good a Colonel as is in the Army of the Potomac. He is full of military, brave but considerate and treats the men like men not dogs as Ames[21] did. He don't say go boys but come. Why! would you believe it he had some breastworks to throw up and what did he do but off his coat and into it himself. I talked with 20 and every man had the same story to tell of their Colonel and his Adjt. who was not afraid to speak to a private.

[19] The Commission provided soldiers with "silent comforters"—a calendar of religious sayings printed in large enough type so that a soldier lying on a hospital bed could read the message for the day.

[20] There were several intense religious revivals during the lull after the battle of Chancellorsville.

[21] Adelbert Ames was Colonel of the Twentieth Maine Regiment until his promotion to Brigadier General on 20 May 1863.

I gave them some lemons and some Bibles. In evening spoke to soldiers of the calmness and adaptability of the Christian religion not a thing of feeling merely but of principle and will, not necessarily boisterous but might be cool deliberation. An every day thing too not of seasons. Good meeting.

Friday 12th.

Took out my basket to the sick men with shirts, jelly, lemons, etc. Heard some cannonading this morning. It is <u>hot</u>; been laying seats in the chapel. In P.M. took out basket and passed the burial of two poor soldiers. Saw the men digging, asked what for. Couldn't tell only detailed to dig according to such dimensions. Then came an ambulance and two coarse boxes were pulled out, ropes attached lowered into the hole, two men took shovels, with pipes in their mouths, in went the dirt. A few, 6, straggling, crippled privates came and looked on. I asked who they were, nobody knew, or where from. No scripture, prayer or hymn, no music, no salute, no military burial or Christian but the mound was finished as it was begun carelessly and so much work was off their hands. I went and sat down on a stump near by and counted the fresh mounds, more than 100. More than a New England grave yard would fill in one's lifetime—all the work of a few days. My mind was attracted by the most beautiful music that came softened by floating over the hills mellowed by the distance. "I feel again life's morning." I thought of Sabino and Penobscot evening rows. I walked over and found the 1st Mass. Cavalry band serenading the hospital as usual. Soon it was the hour for our meeting. I went in and spoke of true courage and exhorted them to make known their feelings before they moved, as their things were already packed and many would be off in the morning, 3 or 4 came out and began the prayers and stated their purpose fully owned to be God's.

Saturday 13th.

Went the usual rounds. Found the wounded already removed and the sick expecting to go. I think many will die on the way. Mr. Small called on me. Stevens[22] and I went out and gathered the remnants. What waste! We found books and clothing and everything not absolutely necessary for personal

---

[22] Henry Stevens, of Blue Hill, Maine, was a USCC delegate. Following the battle, Stevens directed Commission relief work in the Second Division (First Corps) Hospital at Gettysburg.

subsistence cast off. Good books and <u>bad</u> ones. Then went over to the Station and saw our rifle pit that guards the railroad bridge.

It is now the 16th and I must fill up from memory. In the work and excitement of the evacuation, writing was out of the question. Saturday afternoon it became evident that the removal of the sick and wounded meant something for thousands after thousands were placed in cars and the dying even were not left behind. The camp became full of rumors. Ambulances were hurrying in every direction. Soon the rumors took a definite shape. The order as Mrs. McKay gave it to me was to strike tents and remove valuables unless sooner in the hands of the Rebels. We commenced packing. I went to Falmouth for orders and saw it nearly deserted, on the way back I noticed two balloon reconnaissances. Things toward evening grew more and more exciting. A thunder storm came up. Cannonading mixing with the flash and thunder. A whole Artillery Corps came by on the gallop up hill and down. Our things were packed and we on the cars by 8 for Acquia. We were to get through to Washington, if possible. We waited on the wharf expecting transportation and watching our stores till 3 o'clock when I got a chance to finish my sleep in Commission Camp. This was my first experience in the hardships of camp exigencies. The wharf was covered with all classes and conditions of the military sleeping in the damp open door air and hurrying to and fro in the hurry of immediate evacuation. Every instant the rush increased. Cars and ambulances and feet brought in a larger and larger throng all pressing for the next boat.

Sunday 14th.

The longest and hardest "day of rest" I ever had. Getting off goods and packing up at Acquia. Had no regular meals. And such water! Mr. Small told me to make a big X to remember it by. "It needs none," said I. We got a dozen niggers to help us and they kept shirking and embarking afraid of the "rebs". All our goods and stores got in from surrounding stations except Howards, $50 worth, and we got transportation at 4 for Washington. It was hard work to get it, though. Our barge and a canal boat, heavily laden, were towed slowly out of the harbor and I looked back for the last time on the most unhealthy "nasty" place I ever endured. O! said Marden one morning when the Zephers were playing across the marsh. O! for the snuff at a good old fashioned New England skunk. We all agreed. The nail on the head. We passed by the gun boats which were ordered there to cover our retreat and made our way up the Potomac which was covered with similar crafts puffing to Washington and empty back. My nights rest beggars description. The boat was full of soldiers and you could not step round in the dark, in any nook, without stepping on one, it was cold and damp. I should think the sick ones would have died. Mr. Small and I found a little snuggling place on top of some coffins on the upper deck of the canal boat. I soon got stepped on and spit on so much we crawled back and got a box of oranges to sit on which had a convenient crack on it. We were cannibalisticly hungry. Soon he fell asleep on the floor. I crawled under a soldiers bunk.

Monday 15th.

Woke up or rather opened my eyes at Alexandria anchored, took the ferry boat ashore and Stevens and I saw the town and got breakfast. On our journey we distributed two barrels of cakes to the starving soldiers on board. They were frantic for food. Got into Washington at 10. It was a hard sight to see the soldiers exposed on the wharves to the burning sun, waiting for conveyances. I thought I would take a nap on the floor of the Christian Commission rooms and woke up at 4 P.M.

Tuesday 16th.

Stayed last night at Willards,[23] slept. The papers say the Rebels are in Penn. We are working over the boxes in Christian rooms. Called on Hill and saw Strout. Have felt sick exhaustion more than since I left home; feel better now.

Wednesday 17th.

Visited Navy Yard, Georgetown and in eve went to contraband meeting; saw a Negro wedding. Met Dud Haley.[24]

Thursday 18th.

Gave my pass to Charles W. Cort, Norwich Town, Conn't. He promises to return it immediately. Went to Forest Hall,[25] Georgetown, of all the places I was ever in this beats them—dirty, naked, lousy, etc. They were not used

[23] Willards was a popular hotel in Washington, D.C.

[24] Possibly William Dudley Haley, a Bowdoin graduate.

[25] Forest Hall Prison primarily held deserters from the Union Army.

to attention these deserters and how they rushed on us, hands in every direction "please a testament", a hymn book, one of those papers. "Must not give them papers, they have set fire to the building 3 times with them." One Maine man from Orono. I had a call out about this time and said goodby. In P.M. went to Campbell Hospital and found them provided with every luxury and comfort. Beautiful library. So we left and set out for Harwood[26] when the hurricane came up so dusty you could not see 10 feet—then the thunder and lightning and rain and hail, so when we arrived at 3:43, the sides of the Avenue flooded up to the hubs. Boys on rafts were sailing, etc. In eve went to sermons and [the] Metropolitan. A delicious sleep. Had an argument with a Virginian, Rev. Sloane, who told our nigger waiter it was right for the blacks to give us quarters but cut the throat of every Southerner.

Friday 19th.

Got in at 11. Found Rowland Howard here and Rev. Mr. Adams.[27] In afternoon visited hospital and distributed the papers which we left behind in the storm yesterday. First we went to Columbia Col. Hospital and then Mt. Pleasant Hospital. I found a man of the Sixth Maine from Dexter or Guilford, conversed with him, in tears at his unfaithfulness and the remembrance of his home. I wrote his wife for him and also wrote for another man and labored hard till 8 in the evening.

Saturday 20th.

Visited the Guard House, Maj. Cilley[28] and saw them take their baths. In afternoon went down to Georgetown to see Col. Farnham,[29] didn't find

---

[26] Chamberlain visited several Washington area military hospitals, including Harwood Hospital.

[27] Rowland Howard, brother of Major General Oliver O. Howard, was a fellow graduate of Bowdoin College. Howard graduated from Bangor Theological Seminary in 1860 and served as pastor to Congregational churches in Maine, Illinois, and New Jersey. Later, he served as Secretary of the American Peace Society. Rev. Jonathan Adams, a Congregational minister, was a delegate from New Sharon, Maine.

[28] Probably Jonathan P. Cilley of the First Maine Cavalry and a 1858 Bowdoin graduate.

[29] August B. Farnham (1839-1918) of Bangor, Maine, received the rank of Lt. Colonel in the Sixteen Maine Infantry in the spring of 1863.

him. Then visited Aloysius Hospital and Stanton Hospital (Catholic), met a Sister of Charity there. Wrote a letter for sick soldier House and in the evening wrote a letter for a Dane which I shall keep for chirography and orthography.

Sunday 21st.
  Went up to Gr. [Georgetown], saw Farnham, etc.

TODAY IS THE 16TH OF JULY. I have just returned from the front. My notebook being left in Washington carelessly in the suddenness of my departure, I am obliged to fill up a long and adventurous period (the most so of my life) with what scanty notes I can make out in my present unstrung nervous condition. I left here in company of the Rev. Mr. Howard in a mail team for the indefinite "Front" Tuesday, if I remember rightly. I took no baggage with me but two haversacks full of dried beef and hard tack. From every quarter the friends who came out to say goodbye to us, as we were safely aboard, brought us the consoling information the country we were to go through was infested with rebels. Is that so driver? said we somewhat warmly. "O yes plenty of guerillas in that region. They have destroyed our bridges all along the route and we shall have to pick our way along the best way we can." So we passed on over [the] Potomac at long "Chain Bridge" by Arlington Heights and soon found ourselves in "the interior." We found much to interest us through the country seeing the crops and dwellings and customs of the people. We met our cavalry now and then and passed many fortifications guarding Washington. We hurried along in out of the way roads and passes fording streams, etc., till we were soon outside of all sights and sounds of war in a desolate kind of country. On we went meeting nothing, not a team nor footman or soldier for miles. Soon we came to a house and there could be seen inside about 8 men planning; when they saw us they seemed in the most indifferent conversation. We looked on their grey coats suspiciously and all thought of guerillas. We passed unmolested but the subject naturally turned onto guerillas. The mail agent entertained us with tales of how seven straggling soldiers fell asleep and woke up with their throats cut, etc.

  It was getting towards evening and we passed vestiges of plunder and dead horses, etc., which increased a little feeling of uneasiness we had already possessed. I should think we were 30 miles from Washington and had seen no tracks or sound of our soldiers for hours—all of a sudden as we were passing through a long wood we heard an indistinct distant sound—we started again, it seemed to be right near us, halt, drive on says the mail agent, on!, halt (again) or damn you fire and through the loosely hanging cover of our ambulance issued 4 carbine barrels. We halted. I could only see the guns cocked and the hands that held them and hear the trampling of horsemen all around and the clatter of their implements. By this time the curtain was drawn aside and I saw the faces of as hard a squad of cavalry scouters as I ever saw. Where are you bound and who are you? To headquarters, said the agent. To whose headquarters? Gen'l. Howards. He examined papers and then told us he had a Company of the 1st Michigan Cavalry—sent out by Gen'l. Hooker to guard the road, but said he, friends, did you know your danger? The country is full of greybacks here. And you had no business to be on this route. Only last evening, teams were captured here. Fall in the rear and we will give you guard to Dranesville.

We reached Howards HQ. I saw Gen'l. Ames and bore a present from him to Col. of Regt. Major Howard secured me a ride over to the 5th Corps, but said he, did you know that the most risky part of your journey is yet to come? They told of a Chaplain killed and a civilian reporter for N.Y. Times shot on the road the day before between Gum Springs and Aldie. We went 3 miles to Gum Springs and the train did not dare to advance that night.

The next day we ventured and arrived at Aldie.[30] I found the 20th. A Captain was sitting before headquarters. The tent was empty. I looked in, Capt. Spear[31] rose and recognised me in mute astonishment for a moment, etc. The Col. is sick and the Adjt. is down town. Down we went. Met a gay looking horseman cantering up the street. How are you, Adjt? Take off my pants. What will you go for them, a 5 spot?, etc.

Went down to Colonels Headquarters, found him looking poorly, had had a dangerous sunstroke. Saw the Major and spent the night, first, having taken a horse and in company with Tom gone the rounds and seen the battle field where Douty[32] fell. At 3 in the morning in came Adjt., "Col. the order is to be

[30] The Twentieth Maine passed Aldie, Virginia, as they marched north with the Fifth Corps. There was a minor skirmish near there on 17 July 1863.

[31] Ellis Spear was Captain in the Twentieth Maine Infantry Regiment. He later rose to the rank of colonel and commanded the Twentieth Maine Regiment.

[32] Colonel Calvin S. Douty of Dover, Maine, member of the Maine First Cavalry, was killed on 17 June 1863 at Aldie.

ready to move at 4 1/2." We hurried breakfast and I tried in vain to persuade the Col. to take an ambulance for it was raining. He would ride like a man he said. The Commander of 44 took his Regt. along for him. Said by to Aldie forever.

The mud was deep and the marching hard. The streams were swollen and bridges were speedily built by the pioneers. The teams had to ford and the horsemen. One poor fellow got laughed at nicely. His horse threw him into the drink. Teams would get stuck and delayed us. It was along this Goose Creek that Ammy Smith came up and spoke to me. The Col. was advised to go ahead to Leesburg and make himself comfortable. So on we started, drove through the town and put up at a blue stone house—Surgeon Mott's of Confederate Army. Got dinner and polite usage. But they were awful secessionists and we hooked a little Rebel flag there, which was taken from me at Relay House.[33] Our forces came up in 3 or 4 hours and we joined in and were on the march again, refreshed by green peas and ice water, etc. The Col. and I rode along with Col. Rice[34] of 44 N.Y., a splendid chap of Ellsworth Avengers. It was a novel sight to see the fording over the Monocacy. The men stripped and carrying their clothes high in the air, over they went. Our horses sank deep but we saved wet feet by taking the precaution of curling our feet under us. We soon came up to the first estate I have ever seen which filled my idea of old-fashioned Virginia elegance "F. F. V.s"[35] It was the property of Widow Carver. The Munroe Mansion was also very imposing. But before this I ought to have alluded to the charming scenery on the banks of the Potomac at Edwards Ferry. We passed under an arch of trees which shaded the bank, bending to the water—magnificent great sycamores and walnut, five feet through, entwined with grape vines, some certainly 6 inches through. Some had become incorporate into the sycamores, growing up together. We next arrived at Frederick City, which has many beautiful edifices. I found statuary in many private gardens and many signs of old luxury. This city made the strongest demonstrations of Union sentiment of any city I have found in the

[33] Relay House was an important junction of the Baltimore & Ohio and Northern Central Railroads, seven miles from Baltimore, and was usually well-guarded by Federal troops.

[34] Colonel James Clay Rice commanded the Forty-fourth New York Volunteer Infantry Regiment, known as the "Ellsworth Avengers."

[35] First Families of Virginia.

Union South. Flags were flying from every window and everybody honored our troops with a smile or at least a look. How different from the last city Leesburg. All the windows, shutters closed and everything bespeaking contempt for the Yankees. Passing through Liberty, Unionville, Union Mills at Hanover, we met with the first traces of the Rebels. Here were scattered along the road, cart wheels and half burned teams and soon dead horses all along the road and the fences were torn down and the rails laid out at right angles with their former position to convene a cavalry charge. Here had been a gallant little cavalry fight. The grain was trampled thoroughly for a space of a few rods in diameter and the rails were too strong for the horses retreating. They could not leap them and the riders spurring them against them had split the posts down in many places. I should have named the enthusiasm of the soldiers on getting on Northern soil, some near home.

We were having a beautiful march by moonlight from Hanover—the soldiers all full of enthusiasm cheering at every man who noticed them and every nigger when Gen'l. Barnes[36] commanding the Div. announced through Col. Vincent,[37] Actg. Brigadier, that McClellan was appointed to take the Command of Halleck. Then came enthusiasm of a genuine nature. Shout after shout rang upon the air. Everybody said, "it is as good as 50,000 men. It gives new impulse to the Army." The men said, now we will fight. Col. Vincent catching the enthusiasm rode along and with a wave of his hand said, "now boys we will give 'em hell tomorrow."

We pitched that night or more truthfully lay five miles to the rear of Gettysburg. The next morning we advanced and cautiously formed in line of battle and proceeded up the heights a mile to the left of Howard. I remained in the rear with Roland Howard who said it was the best place to see, but before the 5th Corps had pushed into an action, I galloped up to the front as they were still advancing. Shook hands with Col. and Tom and said goodbye—and fell back to the rear amid the whizzing and bursting of shells. Then the clatter of musketry became distinct for a time but it was soon drowned in the terrific roar of cannon on every height, on right and left and the front was one continuous roar and one mass of smoke. I had nothing to eat but a few crumbs of hard bread which I divided with Howard. We were

[36] Brigadier General James Barnes, commander of the First Division, Fifth Corps.

[37] Colonel Strong Vincent, commander of the Third Brigade, First Division, at Gettysburg, died in the battle.

soon out and went in quest of food. All we could get for love or money or entreaty was a few nuts which a gentleman magnanimously proffered us after learning our business and connections. Now gentlemen, I know who you are, walk in, here are some nuts I had laid away for the hogs. Jimmy run into the garret and fetch a bag of nuts. This together with some cherries was all our food for that day—I was also very much exhausted, had to dismount every few hours and take a nap on the ground. I was very sleepy. The next day I was quite sick and faint. I got an old woman to make me a cup of paste. She never heard of gruel and I felt better; that did it for that day together with a small piece of bread the chaplain gave me. I did not feel much like work but there were wounded men pouring in from every quarter, all needing some help, a cup of water or pocket handkerchief. Men without an eye or nose or leg or arm or with mangled head or body would constantly attract your sympathy, each one looking a little worse than the one that went before. I worked principally at the Fifth Corps Hospital where there were fifty from my brothers Regiment—and I scrutinised every new ambulance and every palled stretcher expecting the next would be the Col. or the Adjt. But God had ordained it otherwise. All kind of reports were flying round. The Col. wounded, etc. The men were lying on their backs in the hot sun and it was pouring down terribly. They besought me to shield it from them for the few hours they should live. After a time I managed to do it. When you go to Bangor, Mr. C., exclaimed some voice, see Capt. Jordan and tell him his son—here, the message was interrupted. Others were shouting for help, for water, for soup, for their wounds to be attended to. There came word to me that Capt. Kendall had nothing over him and was entirely destitute of clothes. I managed to get the Chaplain's blanket to put over him to keep the flies off and the cold at night, I worked all that day bringing water, etc. There were a few Rebels I waited on. A Rebel Capt. was very bitter. Before night it became necessary to move the hospital to the rear. So we located it in a beautiful grove a mile back. Here I thought it would be pleasant but a thunder storm came up and it rained furiously and these poor wounded men were throughly drenched. Never mind said they "we are not long for this world." It makes very little difference. I found Lt. Kendall[38] of 20th Maine had not had his wound dressed. The ball was still in his neck. "There it has been for 36 hours" said he. I went around hunting up a surgeon for him

[38] Lieutenant W. L. Kendall died of wounds received on 2 July.

but the 20th had none. The Governor shamefully delayed appointing one, now here were men dying from medical neglect. At last I found an assistant surgeon who kindly volunteered and removed [the ball from] the wound but it was too late–the next I heard from him he was gone. I went to the hospital to carry him his hat which was picked up on the battlefield but the Military symbols were useless to him now, he had entered on his last sleep. He was a patient man.

On the 5th of July I came up to the pickets venturing a call at Hdqtrs. of the 20th. I found all quiet, save now and then an exchange from the pickets. If I ever shook hands heartily, I did so then, as I looked on Lawrence and Thomas alive. I stopped there that night, a rainy disagreeable one. The Col. sick and nervous. It rained, of course, and although we had the unaccustomed luxury of a partial tent over us, it was a pretty uncomfortable night. The next morning the order came to march; the Rebel pickets had fallen back and things looked as if Lee had retreated. We followed up and found such to be the case. We soon reached the heights where the Rebel batteries had been planted. The sight we met with here was fearfully awful. Heaps of horses (artillery) first attracted my attention. They were lying in all positions where they fell. Some were crouched on their legs with heads up and bodies, they looked lifelike.

Soon a uniform at a distance off caught my eye just above the top of the ground, I rode up and here I found the first dead soldier I ever saw on a battlefield. He was lying on his side and frightened my horse as well as startled myself at his hideous aspect. Then, another and another and another. I thought to count them but how little, then, I realized the scenes that were yet to come. The further I rode the thicker the ground was strewn with dead and dying with muskets whole and broken and bent and shattered, with knapsacks and blankets and rubbers, with shells and pieces of shells and shot. And now and then bullets of iron that came from the bursted shells and some of those deadly explosive rifle shot the Rebels use with such deadly effect. When they strike they fly into a thousand pieces all through the body. Here were men of every rank and nation and age. Rebels and Yankees, side by side. Just as they fell in different actions. There were the rough features of the hardy working man and the pale delicate lineaments of the student or the family pet. As I looked on some of these mere boys I thought of their mothers and sisters and dismounting, I picked up letters from their sides, from sisters and fathers and friends at the South. One was dated at Florida and was bitter on the Yankees. I kept them for some time and finally threw them away I had so many things in my pockets. I grew familiar soon with such scenes so that I had the nerve to cut off buttons from the Rebel officers. Soon another man, a soldier, came along and picked their pockets or cut them open and took all he could find. One man got $60 in greenbacks and some Confederate money and a very chaste gold ring (ladies).

The day before I had lost the Col's rubber, at night he complained, said I, tomorrow you shall have one if it costs me $15 to get it. I little thought how I should get one but I felt I should somewhere do so. Here they were scattered all around. I could not refrain to pick up two good ones and a nice new tent which was neatly packed up and lying apart. These things were afterwards sources of much comfort to us—wet nights. But it was not till we reached the heights beyond that the most revolting spectacle met my eyes. It was where the Rebel hospital had been and had been deserted only four hours before. One of the buildings a barn had by some means been consumed, it was still smoking. There were the bones and charred bodies of a large number of men. Some were mere ashes others partly burned. Some soldiers came up and with sticks deliberately went to scraping the burnt bodies where their pockets were supposed to have been in hopes of developing some prize which had withstood the flames. The Rebels in their haste had left many valuables behind, large quantities of soft bread, blankets, knapsacks, caissons containing considerable ammunition, etc. And many religious books were scattered around. It was a noticeable fact that the Rebel soldiers seemed to cling to their Bibles more than ours. A large number of the Rebel dead on the field had open Bibles at their sides and well worn. I remember one was opened at 22 or 21 Matthew. I have in my possession a Rebel hymn book which the Col. picked up then and desired to keep. My attention was attracted to a man lying by himself in a patch of soft plowed ground. I rode across to him, my horse sinking deeply in the mud at every step and I found him with his brains oozing out from a severe wound in the head, soon he gasped and again after a long interval. Finding him still alive we procured stimulants, but his consciousness never returned. We found, also breathing, two of our Army who had been wounded severely and had fallen into Rebel hands. One of them could speak, he said they were treated kindly. There were many of our dead all around, some had been burned with the hospital. The N.Y. Excelsiors were numerous. I shall never forget this battlefield and its surroundings. The house where the Rebel wounded officers were cared for, with the clock still ticking as they left it and the blood on the floors still fresh and everything like cloth blood-smeared and all inside in utter disorder. We found notes written on shingles and paper to the d—d Yankees.

This battlefield, I heard some old veterans say, was the hardest they had seen. I do not care to see another or to smell one. Still we hardened ones managed to eat then, as if nothing unusual was around to disturb us. Our negro servant said he could not go food, so went hungry. The odor was tremendous, overpowering, but the soup was a luxury we did not get every day. To be sure there was no meat in the soup but there were potatoes and onions in it. Just at this time the 6th Corps came by, Major Hyde and Farrar and Chaplain Adams. But I was going. I never shall forget the scenes of that day—the countenances of the men and the positions in which they lay and the ghastly wounds. Some men were headless, some without (legs) limbs, some without bodies. There they were (stretched out) just as they fell or doubled up—in all positions and apparently in all acts. Some reading their Bibles, some getting ready a lunch, some trying to get their blanket over them—but the fatal hour came over them unawares. It is surprising how soldiers bear up. They will never believe their case utterly hopeless. They think "it is not so bad as it seems—I shall get well." I have seen them walking deliberately round with broken skulls, with eyes and part of the face gone, with balls in their bodies and through them. Well, Bill, you got it this time. "Well I reckon, a scratch or so, how do you come off old chap?" They are all very patient and uncomplaining. That evening we moved off, leaving the heights of Gettysburg in the rear and pushed on rapidly after the enemy. The Col. pointed out to me the sunny hillside nook where 20 of his men found their grave in the action of July 2nd. The night came on very dark and we had to make our way through the dense woods in mud and without any path much of the way. Of course, we could not see a hand before us but one could find his way along a road if there were such. The men complained bitterly, lost their way, ran into one another, stubbed their toes and fell with their bayonets against the next man. Were run on by horses and trampled on and horsemen had their heads well beaten by limbs and knots of trees and their legs bruised on huge great trees on either side. Many said it was their hardest march, worse than "stick in the mud." We marched till nearly midnight. Slept on the wet ground and started in at morning.

That days journey brought us to the vicinity of Frederick. Col. and I got good lodgings and breakfast, honey, etc. Here I made up my mind to go to

Frederick and get the Col's. horse shod. I accompanied the troops to the pike and in the most pelting, pouring rain with boots literally full, I made my journey five miles to Frederick city. Here I found a blacksmith's shop. "Shoe my horse, sir?" "Think not!" Urgent case. Officers property, valuable horse hoofs getting destroyed, came miles, propose to shoe him by waiting? Think not. This stupid impudence was all I could get there. At last I was successful. Got it nicely done, went to the Telegraph office and dispatched to Washington for funds on private account. No reply. Waited five hours for orders. None came. Visited hospital to see Major Gilmore[39], just transferred to Baltimore. The long dearth of food and my "abstinence" at Gettysburg made me ferocious at the sight of some hot pies I ran across. 3 and 1/2 satisfied me and a loaf of cake and a tumbler of milk I got afterwards on the road where I stopped to feed my horse for I could get no grain at Frederick.

But I must not omit to state the view we got of Emmettsburg. The Institution of St. Joseph's of such architectural symmetry and immense size and historical celebrity for its convent mysteries and tortures and wiley craft which an escaped nun exposed some years ago, demanded our passing thoughts. It is the Mother Institution of "The Sisters of Charity"[40] you meet with so often in the Southern states. There is only one similar Institution that takes precedence. This is in Paris and is the Mother Institution of the World. The Sisters of Charity are a class of lady devotees who give their lives to virginity and self sacrificing labor and penance. Their dress is a plain black robe and white hood with long projecting flaps,, which slant back in the breeze giving them a very unique appearance. You always see their long string of prayer beads hanging to their side, with gold cross attached to the end. You sometimes meet them with eyes always downcast heading a neat procession of orphan children on a walk. You meet them in hospitals on battlefields, everywhere where acts of kindly service can promote the interests of their Faith which is always paramount. Miss Bunkley in her "Confession of an Escaped Nun" set them forth in an undesirable light, as being cruelly treated and wiley and ostentatious of their humility and self sacrificing devotion and altogether unnatural, unsympathetic, hardened.[41]

But I digress. I was now on the road from Frederick city to the Fifth Corps. The water that had rained into my boots at morning had its traces still there.

---

[39] Charles D. Gilmore.

[40] The Sisters of Charity served both sides as nurses during the Civil War.

I began to feel uncomfortable. I took off one boot as I rode along, hung it over the saddle and then my stocking–then, the other boot–always managing to keep one on so people would see I was not barefooted from want. I could stand it no longer, they didn't dry well, so I drove up to a farm house to dry them. Then I mounted again and reached the 20th at Middletown not feeling in very good trim. That night I was taken violently sick. I vomited all night long, quantities of bile, had a ringing headache and cold chills. They gave me calomel in the morning and sent me to a house, Rev. Dr. Strobel's, to get board till I recovered.–Capt. Keene[42] accompanied me. He sent us to a friend and there I got comfortable quarters for five days. Then I made up my mind to go to Washington, as I was out of funds, and could get no reply to my demands by telegraph and mails. I settled my bill and said goodbye. Got aboard a sutler's team, jolt, jolt till my head hummed again as I stood bent uncomfortably to prevent bumping my head, till five miles of macadamized road was over with and I found myself once more in the city of pies. Here I met Mrs. Fogg of Portland.[43] It was the 14th I think. I left on the train for Washington via Relay House. We passed through a most picturesque country, grand in its hills and streams and cataracts and at the end of four hours ride "Passengers for Washington change cars–Relay House" shouted the Conductor. Out I sprang, saw but one train, a long one, all under steam, full of passengers. Aboard I jumped and saw B. & O. Rail Road over the car door–but we were already whizzing under way. Where does this train go? To "Frederick city, sir." Here, brakeman, this is the wrong train, I want to go to Washington. The accommodating brakeman pulled the string, the car slackened, off I jumped with grateful emotion and made my weary way back again in haste for the Washington train. I met a man, pray sir, has the

[41] Josephine Bunkley's book was part of genre of anti-Catholic literature that received a wide audience before the Civil War. *The Testimony of an Escaped Novice from the Sisterhood of St. Joseph, Emmettsburg, Maryland, the Mother-house of the Sisters of Charity in the United States* (New York: Harper & Brothers, 1855).

[42] Captain Samuel Keene of the Twentieth Maine Regiment.

[43] Isabella Fogg of Calais, Maine, worked as a field nurse for the Maine Camp Hospital Association. Joshua Chamberlain praised her work, writing, "I consider Mrs. Fogg to be one of the most faithful, earnest, and efficient workers in the humane cause in which she is engaged." (Fogg Pension File, National Archives). After a disagreement with its leadership, she became a Christian Commission representative in 1864.

train for Washington gone? No train, sir, tonight, bridge down. This was unpleasant information to a man with 45 cts. in pocket to remain over night on and get supper and breakfast. I hastened to a house for a lunch. They sent me to the tavern. There in an Irish liquor hole, with fighting drunken rows in the other room, I managed to eat a bowl of bread and—what went for milk. I could not stand this for the night. I went out for lodgings. I had not gone far before up came an orderly. Sir, the Captain would like to speak to you at the store below. Thinking he wished to gratify an idle curiosity or to make enquiries about the Gettysburg Battle, I was provoked, tired, and sick as I was to go back. At last the idea came over me that hearing I was on a mission of Charity to the soldiers, he was going to share lodgings with me. I turned and was ushered into the store, where an overbearing puppy with shoulder straps, putting on his official airs, began a series of impertinent questions and cross examinations. I did not care about gratifying the gaping curiosity of a store full of loungers, so after answering his stupid interrogatories till wearied out and disgusted, I handed him my Commission and pass from Gen'l. Patrick, Provost Marshall Gen'l.[44] These he allowed all to read over his shoulders and to scrutinize me suspiciously as he renewed his examination. "I shall give you the trouble to walk over the bridge to Capt. Joseph, Provost for the Relay House district, and there we will have your papers examined and your case attended to. To me the thing looks strange though it may be all right. It is our duty to look up every man and require a satisfactory account."

We reached Capt. Joseph's office. He was an evil looking personage as it is often my privilege to meet. Capt. Stuart introduced "A suspicious person he found prowling around the outskirts. These are his papers." They put their heads together, read and reread my papers compared dates and thought they had discovered a discrepancy. Another set of impudent questions and he concluded that my Commission had a railroad stamp on it he couldn't understand, consequently the papers being suspicious the man who carried them was suspicious and sir you may "consider yourself in arrest." "I shall have to take care of you." What, said I, have you got to do with railroad stamps, your business is to examine our passes and pronounce on the validity of them. Here is my pass from Gen'l. Patrick. If further curiosity, which you have no

---

[44] General Marsena R. Patrick, as Provost Marshal General, was responsible for issuance of all passes within military lines.

right to indulge in, prompts you to know why Gen'l. Patrick gave me this pass—here I show you my Commission on the strength of which I secured this pass and you call it suspicious. You have to resort to a strange expedient when you suspect or pretend to, my loyalty on the ground that the ticket which the R.R. Authorities issued for our Commission and received on the road you cannot understand. General Patrick might not have examined your Commission as thoroughly as I have and it is in my opinion a mysterious document and it is my duty to attend to these things, and if you are a Christian Minister as you profess, you ought to be ashamed to have such papers. I will examine your pockets, take off your boots and shake them. Then he thrust his hands into my pockets—read all my private papers—and notwithstanding an official report of the labors among the wounded at Gettysburg, which I had written to Mr. Demond,[45] he still retained his impertinence—and pretended suspicion. When I took out a little Rebel Hymn book and flag the Col. gave to my keeping, it gave him immense satisfaction. These things he kept and seeing his greedy eye, I remarked, "Sir I shall hold you responsible for the return of all these things." You shall have them in the morning. Now you may call the guard Lt. to convey this man to the guardhouse. Sir, I am unwell. I claim the right at least of decent treatment. I must have lodging in some house, you can station a guard there. My professed position, my health, my connections claim the usual courtesy due a gentleman. As for sleeping in a dirty prison tonight on a board I protest against it. You are no better than I (I used to be a preacher myself and such slang) and a board is none too good for me. Take him up guard. If you persist, can you not give me a rubber to wear out in the rain? You don't need any, it don't rain now, said he putting on his own and getting ready to go out. Off I went gritting my teeth, a bayonet at either ear and a guide front in the rain and mud and darkness up hill and through woods expecting the guard to stumble at every footstep and jab a bayonet through me. We managed to feel our way along about half a mile and arrived. The door opened. A pack of fiends greeted their newcomer, men who had deserted, stolen, murdered and committed all other crimes. They made a ring around me and whispered I was a spy, a Rebel guerilla, a deserter in citizen's clothes and all such. Soon they ventured to ask me and exchange histories and, as I was allowed no

---

[45] Chamberlain wrote this report on 11 July 1863, later printed in an unidentified newspaper found in the Edward Tobey Papers, Massachusetts Historical Society.

blanket or bed, one man offered me a part of his, another generously offered me a piece of raw pork, another some berries which I ate. It was a Rebel deserter, a cousin of Morgan.[46] I laid down on a board with a corner of my new companions blanket which smelled some, as well as the rest of things and the building generally. I had never, but once at Forest Hill prison in Georgetown, seen such filth, such dirty men, such confusion. Men were cursing, shouting, playing cards all night. My neighbor would sleep ten minutes or lie, then with a yell he would up and grab the next man by the hair, they would scuffle and howl and then someone in the other corner would catch the spirit—vulgarity, oaths, songs, dancing, picking lice, spitting tobacco juice and snickering was the order of the night. I lay there in the filth, with eyes open all night—till the cold damp air was pouring upon my head and with nothing over me and a very small edge of the blanket under me for I did not care for too close proximity to my naked neighbor. I began to feel chilly. I could not stand it. I rose, and tried to get out the door by the guard with his bayonet, for a breath, and other conveniences unmentionable. You can't go out here, others were passing in and out but I was under special restrictions, finally seeing the absurdity, he allowed me to go to the corner of the building. The milk maids and peddling women were just coming up with their morning stores, but nature before convention. They must look the other way. I returned after buying a drink of milk, which almost turned my weak stomach and enquired for bread. After much importunity and long waiting, they sent me my morning rations. I had taken a mouthful when in came an orderly looking up the suspicious civilian and ordered me immediately to the Depot for the morning train to Baltimore. This was what I longed for, I threw away my bread and with a light heart was bayoneted down through the crowds of gaping soldiers to the Depot. Here I was presented to my Lord Mogul again. I greeted him with a look. He gave me one. It was 7 o'clock. He knew I was anxious to be sent to Baltimore. I had remarked to him when he informed me it was his purpose to send me there, that that was all I asked for, an opportunity to have an intelligent man glance at my papers. But I must wait his official ease. The train came and passed. O! How it nettled me. Four more hours before another. I waited in silence giving him one of my looks once in awhile. I asked for my property, said he,

[46] Confederate General John Hunt Morgan led a notorious raid into Ohio and Indiana in July 1863.

"it will all be sent to Baltimore with you but the Rebel flag—that is missing." I remembered my thoughts and remarks the night before. Said I, if you dare to retain any of my private property or that in my keeping, there will be trouble. None of your impudence. I have the right to arrest a Devil or a Saint, and I will let you know now it is my opinion you belong to the former class. What right have you to carry round that flag? I love the flag of my country. Too many men such as you is what caused the trouble at N.Y. You ought not to run at large. "I shall report your treatment at Baltimore." "You will get treated as a spy deserves at Baltimore, don't flatter yourself that you can get out of this easily." Ha! We will see. The train came. I asked him before I left for his card. He colored and refused but said, "Sir, I back up all my acts—I have authority." A Lieut., with sword in hand all the way, took me to Baltimore on the train together with another soldier. We went to the Provosts. He read the letter Capt. Joseph had accompanied with my documents. The Lt. took him aside and told him some additional privacy. I didn't know what might after all be hatched out of lies. I for the first time began to fear. The Provost said he was ready to attend to Mr. Chamberlain. The guard had vanished. He went to the desk, opened my Commission, glanced at it, passed it to me and without a question said, "I see no trouble with your papers" Said I, "Can I get a pass to Washington." O yes. He returned my papers. I found the pass from Patrick missing. The villain at Relay House had retained it for the sake of carrying his point. I cared more for the flag. Said I, Joseph has arrested me through an overbearing love of authority and ignorant officiousness. He has treated me shamefully and retained property of mine. You have a right to complain of him. No officer has a right to retain any property in such a way or of such a nature. I looked round Baltimore for Major Gilmore, could not find him, had fifteen cents in my pocket and had just learned that the train for Washington did not leave again till 4. What should I do for something to eat. I did not dare to venture out into a respectable saloon with my fifteen cents. So I picked out the cheapest looking place I could see and found a piece of ham with an egg on top, price ten cents. This was providential. I felt my mouth water. I purchased—one mouthful and I had my attention suddenly attracted to the back window. What was in my mouth went into my hand. What was in my hand went out the window. I could go mule meat at the front as a part of the romantic experience of war but to eat mule meat in Baltimore City—it was too tame, altogether common-place. I could not bring myself to it—too fastidious for that. The other 5 was precious. A woman came in just then from the country. I thought of country prices and examined her nice blue berries. I got a paper full, went to the Depot to rest. Every chair and bench and box was occupied. I got a shrewd idea into my head just then. There was the car where I could lie down and need not fear to get left, for I knew I should fall asleep as soon as I found a seat—I stowed myself comfortably aboard—was congratulating myself over my cunning when lo! a surly voice "nobody allowed in these cars till tickets are sold." When will that be? "Two hours." So out I came and the man locked the car behind me and threatened the man that prowled round those cars any more at such unconscionable hours. I had learned to respect authority from no matter how low or ignorant a source, so I did not debate with the Irishman. At the appointed hour the cars started and I consoled myself that though penniless, soon I should be in Washington where I had ample funds. I had left them there and took with me to the front only what I considered immediately necessary for I expected to be taken prisoner going through guerilla country. On went the cars till the familiar locality of the Relay House attracted my attention. Looking out the window, whom should I see strutting through the Depot but the identical "Mogul", he didn't seem to recognize my countenance. "Capt!" he looked the other way "Capt! I say you have given me some trouble now perhaps I can return the favor." We exchanged glances and goodbye forever. I shall report him yet, as soon as I learn the proper steps. The cars had now reached Annapolis Junction but here we waited and started and backed and waited till everybody got impatient, one hour, two, three, then we got off again, went a few miles and waited again, found we had to change cars—the bridge was destroyed. This took another hour to change baggage and all for some distance round the bridge. All aboard but then we had to wait again, nobody conceived why. Soon the news came that the engine was out of order, so we had to await the arrival of another from Washington.

Suffice it to say we arrived at Washington at twelve at night. Stopped at hotel St. Charles and in early morning slipped out and thanked God for the Christian Commission, as I found myself there and my hands on my valise that contained funds and if ever a man felt flush and independent it was I, as I strutted into St. Charles picking my teeth and with $25 in pocket, called with an indifferent air for "my bill." This ends my eventful journey to the Front and lands me again at Washington and brings me back to where I began after the 16th of June. The next Monday I went to Camp Convalescent near

Alexandria via Aqueduct bridge and Arlington House. Here adventurous life ends and I am peacefully engaged in religious and charitable labor. We are having quite a revival, scores come forward every night and kneel for prayers. Here Phillips labored. At Washington last week I was treated courteously by Cols. friend Mrs. Harris. Also Honorable Mr. French, 20th Auditor, urged me to dinner with him and showed me the beautiful sword he had purchased for Gen'l. Ames. I left this space to be condensed, so I finish this at home Aug. 3rd. I arrived at Camp C.,[47] Monday, 20th, didn't like location neither the air of the place nor the air of the person, Mr. Graves, who wanted to see a man before he came and advised me to go to Washington. I went! He explained, I said "good morning" but I guess I won't go back I "resigned my Commission." I concluded to go the "front." Got my pass and thought better of it and made arrangements to steer for N.Y. Saw my Jew friend and heard from Shearer[48] at the last moment. Got on the track of my money but all my clothing, shirts, handkerchiefs, collars, hat, gloves, etc., etc., were never more brought to light. Green Delegate! Don't carry your nice clothes to the front, they are so much more useful in Washington! I think I see some poor private adorned with my fine linens and dignified with my long dress coat, going on his way rejoicing and blessing the liberality of the Christian Commission.

I left Washington joyfully Saturday, 25th, reached N.Y. Sunday morning, spent two days there at 5th Avenue Hotel, rode over to Central Park, saw Barnhams Museum,[49] got a fine view of the moon through a good telescope, very fine. Arrived in Boston, Tuesday. Stopped at Aunt's arranged business with Mr. Demond, $42 and started for Portland at 3. There I called at Mr. Merrill's and on Mr. Keene of 20th Maine. Then home by Webster and found Tom already here—but mother sick. Was glad to reach the old homestead once more and settle down in luxurious ease to contemplate the events of the season which never will be forgotten and need not the help of this note book to be recalled. ✢

[47] Camp Convalescent was a hospital outside Washington, D.C.
[48] Frederic Shearer was the Christian Commission's Washington agent.
[49] Phineas T. Barnum's Museum in New York City.

Christian Commission Station, Camp Letterman

LIBRARY OF CONGRESS

An Incident at Gettysburg

✤ ✤ ✤ ✤ ✤ ✤ ✤

Jane Boswell Moore

FROM EARLY 1861 until the end of the war, Jane Boswell Moore worked tirelessly as a relief agent with the Union army. Goldsborough C. Griffith, president of the Maryland Christian Commission, described her as one of the "most energetic spirits I ever knew." He said, "Miss Moore...has visited every Hospital in our District besides a large number in Virginia. She understands the business thoroughly." After the war, General William Emory, who knew Jane and her mother from their work in the Shenandoah Valley, said, "The names of Miss and Mrs. Moore are on the lips of thousands to whom they have ministered in camp and hospital."[1]

Yet, few history books record her name and we know little about her personal life. According to Baltimore City Directories, Dr. William Boswell Moore was an Irish-born physician who ran an apothecary shop with Charles H. Moore, apparently a brother. The 1850 Census lists Dr. Moore in Baltimore's Sixth Ward, with his wife, Jane C. Moore, aged thirty-five, and her daughter, Jane, aged eight. He died in 1854. The portrait, then, is of an educated young woman, only nineteen or twenty, when the war begins. According to social propriety, she is accompanied almost everywhere by her widowed mother.

Following the battle of Manassas, she visited local hospitals, joined by her mother. She recalled, "...even as we heard convalescing patients allude to the battle-fields—I fainted. But they said our sympathy cheered them, and after a determined struggle our visits were constant."[2]

---

[1] G. C. Griffith to William Boardman, 28 March 1863. USCC Papers, National Archives.

[2] Frank Moore, *Women and the War* (Hartford, Connecticut: S. S. Scranton, 1866), 556.

In the month before the battle of Gettysburg, the Moores labored near the camps of the Army of the Potomac in Virginia. In late June, Reverend Jonathan Adams, a Christian Commission delegate from Maine, encountered the mother and daughter at Fairfax courthouse where he helped them to distribute literature brought from Baltimore. Later, all three worked in the Second Corps hospital at Gettysburg.[3]

The mother and daughter team continued their work, spending early 1864 in hospitals near Winchester, Virginia, then moving to Point of Rocks near Petersburg. By the end of the war, her health had been "seriously impaired by the hardships she suffered, and by the agitations of those four years of unremitting military service."[4]

Moore was a gifted writer. At the beginning of the war, when her hometown of Baltimore divided its loyalties, she wrote blistering letters to a local newspaper, condemning secession. Later, she contributed children's stories to the *Lutheran Observer*, a religious newspaper published in Baltimore. Beginning in the fall of 1862, Jane Boswell Moore wrote frequent columns on her relief work for the *Observer*.[5]

The Moores illustrate the role of women in the Christian Commission. They never received appointments as delegates, yet they saw themselves as part of the organization. Jane referred to herself as a delegate and wrote heartfelt appeals for contributions to the organization. The mother and daughter worked outside the Commission's chain of command yet served alongside delegates and drew upon the USCC's supplies. Her essay, "An Incident at Gettysburg," comes from the *Second Annual Report* of the Maryland Committee of the Christian Commission. ☩

[3] Jonathan Adams Diary, Special Collections, Bowdoin College.

[4] Frank Moore, *Women and the War*, 570.

[5] "Miss Jane Moore," *Lutheran Observer*, 26 December 1862.

ABOUT THREE MILES from Gettysburg, across the fields southwest of the Baltimore pike, is a spot which will long be remembered by those who witnessed the awful scenes which transpired there after the battle. For more than four weeks (beginning the first few days after the fight) we were engaged in the field hospitals of the Second Army Corps, which, with every other, and perhaps more than any other, covered itself with immortal glory on that bloody field. Words utterly fall short in describing the appearance of those woods on the morning we reached the hospital, after riding through swollen streams, amid the still unburied bodies of men and horses that lay putrefying on the field.

The site of the hospital, which had been hurriedly chosen, was in a grove of trees on a piece of rising ground, surrounded nearly on all sides by a ravine, along which ran a creek, near whose banks lay hundreds of wounded and dying Rebels, most of whom were exposed to the pitiless pelting of the storm. Such a thing as a cot, a bed, or a stretcher, was scarcely to been seen—protected from the damp earth only by a blanket, the wounded lay on all sides, ours mostly under the shelter of large tents—but a few rods distant thirty or more interments were daily taking place, each day's dead being wrapt in their blankets and laid at the tent door until time could be found to remove them. Shrieks, cries and groans resounded on all sides, not only from those in the tents, but on the amputating tables, which were almost constantly occupied; and who could pass them without a dreadful shudder at those ghastly bleeding limbs heaped without, which the eye, however cautious, could not always avoid? Is it not well sometimes to pause and think at what an awful cost our country was then and there redeemed? Never will those scenes of suffering pass away; with terrible reality and vividness we feel that they must dwell in our memory forever!

Among many touching incidents, I find in my journal a hurried record of one especially to which I now look back with a feeling of mournful satisfaction. It was that of Samuel Parish, of the 28th (Rebel) Virginia Regiment. After a week spent in unabated efforts to supply the needy of both sides, who were at first in a very different condition from that which has afterwards been described, we were one afternoon on our way to take a cup of coffee with the Surgeon of the 2d Pennsylvania, when a citizen came from the new Rebel encampment, on a gentle slope of ground directly back of our tent and beyond the hollow, and mentioned the fact that a Rebel boy who was in a dying condition wanted some one to talk with him about Jesus. I went at once, and to a shelter-tent on some straw, his grey blanket thrown aside, lay a lad of nineteen, shot through the lungs, and breathing with great difficulty. The man said he had found some one who would talk with him. "I am very glad," he said, turning to me, "that you have come." Seating myself on a log in front of his tent, I began by making some inquiries as to his condition and history. He told me he had been in the army twelve months; that whilst away at Suffolk his mother had died, but he spoke of a young sister to whom some one had written. He had never been wounded before, and when I remarked, "This will about end your battles, are you aware of it?"

He answered, "Oh, yes, I know that before to-morrow's sun rises I shall be gone, and I should be glad to rest if I were quite sure I would go to heaven."

"And why should you not be sure? The way is very clear—the Saviour makes no hard condition, but as the hymn says,

'Tis only look and live.'

Now tell me what it is that troubles you and let me see if I can do you any good? You do not doubt the Saviour's word, do you?"

"Oh, no, ma'am, but its temptation; I think, yesterday, I felt as if I was saved and happy, but today something says you don't feel just as you ought, and so I am cloudy and unhappy."

Fixing my eyes on him earnestly, I said, "Samuel, what is it that saves us—is it our feelings or anything that we have done or can do?"

"Oh, no, but I am tempted to believe I am not so great a sinner and then I don't feel my sins as I ought."

"And probably in your weak, dying state you never will feel them so. None of us realize such things as we should, but it is a blessed thing that the Lord Jesus does not require of us any thing more than to feel our need of Him and be willing and ready to take him as our Saviour. Feelings are little to be depended on. What you want now is simple faith—faith in the power of the Lord Jesus to save you, and faith in His willingness to do so; but let me read to you a little narrative of the death of a soldier whom I knew, and I trust his happy words may be yours."

I then read the little soldier's tract, "He is my Christ." At the words "Remorse, grief, and tears will not save you," he said, "Oh, no!" and when I read further, "Will you not have this Christ for your Saviour?" he almost sprang from his humble couch exclaiming in a deeply fervent tone, and with an emphasis I never shall forget, "I will!" then, adding in broken sentences,

"Oh, Lord, receive me! Oh, Lord, accept me at once—just right away—let me feel it now! Be with me when trouble is near!"

I explained to him more fully the plan of salvation, its wonderful freeness, the helplessness and guilt of the sinner more fully, saying you must just go to Christ because you are weak, and He is strong, you must trust in His righteousness because you are sinful and He is holy. "I see it," he exclaimed.

> *Here, Lord; I give myself away,*
> *Tis all that I can do.*

"That is all that is needed; now trust your soul with Jesus, and feel happy in Him. You know His word can never be broken; and it says, 'Believe on the Lord Jesus, and thou shalt be saved.'"

"But," he replied, "it troubles me to think I can't pray. I can't even think a sentence, and if I do, it's all wrong."

"Well, you can say, Lord forgive my sins, and save me for Christ's sake, and, if you can't do that, trust your soul on Him. He never yet cast out any poor soul that came to Him, and He never will. You remember reading, 'He is able and willing to save unto the uttermost all that come unto God by Him.'"

"No, ma'am, I never had any schooling. I worked with my father and brother-in-law harvesting, for we were very poor, and I had a hard time of it; so we calculated that I would get my schooling when I was above size; but then this war broke out, and now that's all done with." I asked if he remembered that sweetest of hymns, "There is a fountain filled with blood," which seems to express the penitent emotions of the believer in all ages, and his eye brightened as I said, "What a comfort it is to know that this fountain is open for you, and that in it you can lose all your guilty stains."

He then asked me to draw his socks on his feet, as the fleas troubled him, making me promise to come again that afternoon. Entering other tents I witnessed scenes of heart-rending agony. A North Carolinian, whose leg had been amputated, and who was now suffering from lock jaw, was very anxious for a drink, and also to be turned over. We tried in vain to get a bottle or glass to his mouth; his teeth were set and his agony fearful, but he continued feebly to articulate "Oh, do get the doctor to come here a minute, and I will do anything for you." The nurse said the man could not be moved, but would probably die before morning. I have witnessed much suffering, but thought then that I had never seen anything so truly heart-rending. That piteous, agonized face, shall I ever forget?—his breast heaving convulsively with the death struggles.

He spoke of a chaplain who had been there and was gone; so I went for one of the Christian Commission, who remained with him. Later in the afternoon I again saw Samuel, and read to him the tract called the "Sick Soldier," and also, prayers and verses from the Soldier's Manual of Devotion. His lips moved as I read, and most fervently at the close did his voice join in the words "for Christ's sake." He listened most attentively, not wishing me to begin until he had adjusted every fold of his blanket, "because," he said, "I want to hear it all." On leaving him, he said, "I shall be gone in the morning." "I hope not, but if so, I hope you will be with Jesus. I want you to give yourself to Him, and not think about feelings or anything else that will cause you to doubt."

"I will," he said, and, bidding me "good night," covered himself with his blanket and turned over for that long last sleep, from which, if I see him on waking, it will be on the resurrection morning. Next day I came again, but the poor North Carolinian was dead, and I saw a group around Samuel's tent. They told us he was dead, but I saw he was perfectly unconscious and dying, slowly struggling for breath, which he continued to do nearly all day.

Exciting Scenes.

Teams were accordingly sent, and we rode out over the battle field passing Cemetery Hill and the yet unburied bodies of some poor Rebels. Riding on through muddy roads and swollen streams to the tents of the First and Second Army Corps, against whose undaunted front Lee's army massed in one last great effort, language fails to depict the misery which was everywhere present. Scarcely had one man out of a thousand anything more than the ground, covered with an old blanket or an oil cloth, to lay on, and hundreds had undergone amputation since the battle. Miserable little shelter-tents alone protected them from the rain, whilst numbers of the poor wretched Rebels had not even these, but were exposed through all the heavy rain of Tuesday night, with scarcely covering enough to keep warm in dry weather. All were clamorous for bread and butter; our own men were badly off; the Rebels begged piteously; the doctors were busily engaged in amputating; great piles of limbs being heaped up at the three different tents, and hundreds were suffering to have their wounds washed and dressed. The air at times resounded with moans and shrieks of anguish; men were employed all the time as grave diggers, and the dead lay at tent doors on the ground, as well as on the bloody stretchers, waiting burial.

We set to work immediately, buttering bread, making lemonade, changing bloody clothes for clean ones, giving out wines, brandy and towels. Could loyal Baltimore have witnessed the suffering, we are sure that hundreds of men and women possessed of energy and endurance would volunteer, bringing with them hundreds of loaves of bread, butter, wines, brandies, soup, eggs, lemons, oranges, &c. We had many delegates on the ground, and yet how unequal to meet the wants of so vast a number. It was heart-rending to see the friends of those killed and wounded in search of them. One poor widow from Philadelphia, with five little children dependent upon her exertions as seamstress, came this evening to look for her eldest son. She had heard he was dead, but could not believe it. On reaching the hospital she was told he waited in one of the tents. "Oh!" she said, "how my heart beat for joy, but when I went in, they told me he was dead."

He had written to her that nothing would induce him to miss this battle, as on it depended the fate of Pennsylvania, and perhaps the whole country. During the battle he raised his head from behind a *stone* wall to fire, and being shot through the head, was instantly killed. Oh! said the poor mother, if I could only know he was prepared. Alas! in the hurry and difficulty of supplying the temporal wants we have little time to whisper to the dying of Jesus, or point them to Christ, upon whom so many poor Rebels were calling most piteously for help. Physical anguish forced from many, cries of "Oh, Lord, have mercy!" "Oh, my Heavenly Father, pity me!" We have no space to dilate upon the horrors that we have seen. Before to-morrow's sun rises scores of human beings on both sides will have passed into eternity.

In the true spirit of Christianity we are laboring for both sides. They lie *side* by *side*, many without even a straw under them, some with a rail or bottle under their head, half clothed, destitute and suffering; many carried fresh from the amputating table.

A lieutenant from Virginia, dying of lock-jaw, having lain out in the rain after his leg was amputated, seemed exceedingly happy, and took great delight in hymns, which, he said, just expressed his feelings. He told his brother, who leaned over him in an agony of grief, to tell his mother and sisters to meet him in heaven. Taking his brother's place, I said, while fanning him, "Lieutenant, do you remember that beautiful hymn, 'There is a fountain filled with blood?'"

His eye lighted as I slowly repeated it, and "Jesus, lover of my soul," pausing after each, to see that he was neither dead nor sleeping I then repeated that sublime hymn, "Rock of ages, cleft for me," and as I was then obliged to leave him, read the closing verse, endeavoring to throw into those glorious words all their full strength and force of meaning. It is impossible to describe the beam of glory, unearthly and beautiful beyond all that I have seen, which lit up his face as I proceeded. His eyes shown with brilliant lustre; he pressed my hand affectionately, seeking to detain me, laid his head for a moment on his breast, and then pointed upward, as though he would have contrasted here and there.

And truly marvellous was the contrast. Earth here with its scenes of blood and carnage; its din of strife, its bloody battle-fields, on which the roar of cannon and bursting shells have lately died away; its acres of graves; its long rows of tents with their suffering inmates; and war, with tens of thousands of desolated homes and broken hearts; side by side with all this rose before him in peaceful contrast the quiet rest of that heavenly city with its angel throng, composed of the saints and martyrs and believers of all ages evermore singing the praise of God. All these seemed to pass before him, and he looked up as the glorious prospect was revealed to his dying gaze.

Pleasing Recollection.

"What do you take me for?" I asked, laughing, "a pedler or a secesh?" In Maryland, people think it only right to do all they possibly can for the soldiers, not only at home, but abroad; and as the sick in Baltimore are well attended, we came down to the Rappahannock, thinking there was more to be done here. We find great pleasure in doing it. We can never pay our soldiers for the sacrifices and hardships they undergo for us, but we "*do want to show them we are grateful.*"

"Those are the words soldiers like to hear," was the enthusiastic reply. "We hav'nt heard such words down here, I can tell you."

"No," I said, "of course you would not expect; the people are Rebels."

"Well," said another, "we have one pleasant recollection to carry away with us from the Rappahannock."

A Life Saved.

A lad from Hagerstown, named Luther Cridler, interested us very deeply; he lay perfectly unconscious, on a rude straw pallet, in that dull, heavy stupor which we had seen in so many cases of typhoid fever. We wiped the moist brow, forced the closed teeth open, and the lips being held apart, poured a few spoonfuls of brandy and water down his throat. Then leaving the bottle in charge of a faithful comrade for his use, and filling canteens with lemonade, they bade them all "good bye." From the friend who stood by us at Luther's side they learn how much he was benefitted by the gift of Mr. Eichelberger. "Indeed," he writes, "by it I think his life was saved."

In reading the following from a letter from Baltimore to a friend, "Do not spare any pains in advancing the cause—you shall not want for anything—Let us know if you are in want, and it shall be forwarded immediately." I could not repress the exclamation, "That is dear old Baltimore forever! Surely a blessing will come upon our people for what they have done in behalf of these wounded and dying men." And has not a blessing come upon us already in the preservation of our homes and loved ones from impending destruction? No human pen can adequately depict the horrors of a battle-field. Here in this hospital—we see manly forms maimed and wounded in every imaginable way. In going round with the fresh eggs you sent, and which were most invaluable, it was no uncommon thing in asking at the door of each tent for the amputated cases (as we had a limited supply. we could not spare them to others) to receive the nurse's reply, "I have ten in this tent who have each lost a limb." And oh! how many grateful thanks we receive—how many soldiers bless Baltimore, and will forever vindicate her loyalty. And the poor Rebels, too, are most grateful. Pitiful, indeed, are the histories of the privates, forced in and openly acknowledging that they have no sympathy with the cause they are in. It is dreadful to see them daily losing life and limbs with such bitter regret. "Bad enough in a good cause," said one, "but, oh it is so hard in a bad one." We have men from almost every state, both North and South. Within the last day or two the Rebels have been put under little shelter-tents. Previous to this, when we were unable to procure tents, a number of them lay on the slope of a hill, with a dirty blanket and oil cloth under them. We have had very heavy rains, and they were, of course, much exposed.

Unprepared to Die.

One poor, bright-eyed boy, whose leg had been amputated, and who will probably die in a few days, interested us deeply. He told us his name was James Whitson, from Virginia; that he was on a visit to Norfolk when he was conscripted and taken away; and, said he, with quivering voice and tearful eyes, "I never saw my father and mother since." He thought he would soon get well. As I leaned over him, to supply his wants, I said, "Your leg looks badly; if you should not get well, James, are you ready to die?" He looked up gravely—his dirty, grey felt hat slouched over his face—(those grey hats that we have seen on battle-fields where the wearer had lately fallen)—and said, "No, m'am, I am not prepared."

Relief to the Dead.

Day before yesterday it rained very hard; I took a bottle of brandy and tin cup and went down the hill-side, where the wounded Rebels lay exposed to the storm, giving to each a small quantity of brandy and water. They were thinly clad and excessively cold, but they knew that many of our own men were suffering as much, and were very thankful. I went up to one, whose face was partially covered with a blanket. I thought to protect him from the rain; "Friend, won't you have a little of this to keep you from feeling the cold?" He made no reply, and I repeated the question, but drawing the cover away saw that life had fled. Most deeply have I felt for them. They seem very anxious about themselves.

Pray for the Dying.

One died yesterday whose leg had been amputated. A few minutes before his death I went in to see him. "Oh," he said, "lady, pray." I said, "Put all your trust in Jesus—are you resting on Him?" He said, "Yes." I have often in going in and out of his tent heard him feebly ejaculating to himself, "Oh, Lord, help me. Lord, do forgive me!" I doubt not that that blessed Saviour heard the cry of this poor creature, away from home, thus struggling with death.

Take Me Home.

A Captain from Indiana, with closed eyes, was earnestly praying aloud, "Jesus, take me to thy home! Jesus, take me to thy bosom! Lord, have mercy on me!" Before the morning breaks the bosom of Jesus will be his last and most blessed resting place.

Letter from Gettysburg, 26 July 1863
THE LUTHERAN OBSERVER, 21 AUGUST 1863

Yesterday (Sabbath) was a very warm day. In the morning we rode to town in an ambulance to procure some stores, and on our return visited the thirteen tents entrusted to our care. These contained some sixty or seventy wounded rebels now in separate tents, for although we of course would have preferred ministering to our own and, still owing to this preference on the part of many, there was a certainty they would suffer, we were quite willing to attend them. And grateful suffering creatures we found them; many say that our kindness has done more to subjugate them than all the shells and balls that have been fired during the war,—they never expected such treatment, and have not the heart to raise a hand against us.

Only a few days after the battle, one who had laid out in the storm told us that he never would forget our kindness; "and," said he, "if I only knew how to keep from going into the army again, I would not go." I answered that he could readily avoided by taking the oath, and remaining within our lines.

"But," said he, "then in sixty days I would be taken into your army, and seeing there is no escape, I might as well fight with my own people as not, though if I could, I would give up fighting altogether."

I told him I was not aware of any such fact, nor did it exist, on which he and his neighbor were very much astonished, the one remarking, "You see, Jim, they tell us what ever suits their purpose."

I have endeavored with the box you sent to supply every man in our hospital with a little book, which the rebels said were now very scarce in the South. One, a fine intelligent fellow, asked me to take a piece of ticking, and make a little bag like a haversack, in which he could carry *his* home. This man had been a member of the Methodist church for ten years, and greatly enjoyed the hymns in the soldiers' hymn-book.

A North Carolinian said I would hardly believe him if he were to tell me all he had undergone. With but little to eat, he had to march hard and fight hard, tramp twenty or thirty miles, with no rations but a few crackers. Officers were so tyrannical, they would not even allow them to take a drink as they ran along.

I remarked, "Were they afraid you would desert?"

"Yes, I suppose so. This was the worst whipping we ever got; Antietam was bad, but nothing to this. Plenty of us wanted to desert then as we were coming into Maryland, but they told us the bushes were full of Yankees who were waiting to shoot us, and would not show us a bit of mercy, but cut us right down."

"Did you not know that some of your companions got away?"

"Yes, we knew that a good many left us as we came over the mountain, but we never heard of them, and thought they had been shot."

Wishing to keep up their spirits, I remarked playfully to one, "How foolish it is in me to be feeding you and strengthening you to fight against us?"

"Well, if you do," rejoined one, "I'll do it on one leg." Another said, "Don't blame us. War is not what it is cracked up to be. We did not want to come, but it wasn't for us to say whether we would stay or come."

Oranges have been very scarce. Yesterday we gave one to a poor rebel, who had been craving one all day. He afterwards showed it to a friend, saying that he would not take a dollar for it.

Nearly every day wives, mothers, sisters and friends visit the hospital for the purpose of finding the grave and bodies of their loved ones who have fallen in the strife, so that our sympathies are not only enlisted for the wounded and suffering, but also in behalf of their sorrowing friends. The other evening a lady came in search of her husband, but she was too late, as he was dead. "Oh," she said, with tearful eyes, "he talked so of me and his little lame girl." Then in a perfectly girlish woman came all away from Maine on a three days fruitless journey, the New York rioters having cut the telegraph wires, so that the second dispatch announcing his death did not reach her. And how, on her return, she was dreading to meet his aged, poor and feeble parents. His father was scarcely able, from rheumatism, to carry his food to his mouth, and his mother had never recovered from injuries received from being thrown out of the wagon. She said the Maine women would be out to help the soldiers but they were so far away, and the newspaper accounts were very different from the reality—in the little village where she lived they had raised since the battle eleven hundred dollars. I mentioned in a former letter our change of hospital, the new location been much more healthy and pleasant. The tents extend round the edges of a beautiful clover field, a little below witch, in a grove near a brook, are the tents of the Commission and numerous other parties. Just at present, as the cool air is surging delightfully through the trees, the view presented to our gaze is a very pretty one. In front is the waving clover still wet from last night's rain, and the white sun-lit tents relieving a background of dark gray clouds. In the distance looms the summit of Round Top, the frightful rocky position whose strength gained the day for our forces. Below is a ravine, over which the rebels crossed in their vain attempts to take our batteries. Their graves are thickly strewn, but many in unburied form is stretched on the rocks and near the brook.

In one spot on the battlefield are three or four broken down pieces of artillery, struck and disabled, whilst flying across the field—the open boxes lie here half filled with missiles of death. We counted about one hundred unexploded shells, thus arrested in the work of destruction.

And here on the great plain where the tide of battle surged like an angry sea, is the spot where Lee's last great effort was made to break through our lines, and surely the spot tells of the struggle; a little beyond we see the woods where the rebels formed, led by Lee, Longstreet, and Hill, ere they made their final charge, on which depended the fate of Maryland and Pennsylvania. We walk around the little stone wall or breastwork, which stretches across the wide plain, and feel that we walk here in safety, only because our men stood their ground, even though the foe leapt the wall and seized their guns, *they stood their ground indeed.* But the hillock of graves—the little forest of headboards scattered everywhere, and there over the battlefield, the piles of empty haversacks, the caps and blue coats everywhere, and guns used by hands now cold in death, seemed to tell with mute eloquence at what an awful price Maryland and Pennsylvania were redeemed!

Oh how must they not have struggled along the wall, where coats, hats, canteens and guns are so thickly strewn; beyond it two immense trenches filled with rebel dead, and surrounded with grey caps, attest the cost to them. The earth is scarcely thrown over them, and skulls with ghastly grinning teeth appear, now that the few spadefuls of earth are washed away. In these trenches when they plainly see the rise and swell of human bodies; and oh how awful to feel that these are brethren—deluded and erring, yet brethren. Surely, no punishment can be too great for those whose mad ambition has filled these graves!

A Leaf from the Past
THE LUTHERAN OBSERVER, 26 FEBRUARY 1864

I write these lines in the solitude of my chamber, on the eve of the National celebration at Gettysburg. Gettysburg! Can I ever hear that name without a thrill of indescribable emotion? A great throng is assembled in the square of the Diamond, and the bands are playing without. The diamond! What associations are called out by the words, and how utterly unconscious coming generations will be, aye, even gazing years hence, of the scenes enacted there after that memorable struggle. They living only in the present will not use the streets as we have done, will not know that this pavement was filled with rusty bayonets and muskets gathered in the field and dropped from the grasp of the fallen, will not realize the grief of that poor heart-stricken widow, whose manly son, her pride and staff, had fallen, as she stood by me gazing sadly on the mute yet eloquent site said, "I suppose my boy is there!" They will not know how foot-sore and weary she traversed that immense field of slaughter, seeking for one mound in which, bloodstained and cold lay her firstborn, nor know how my heart bled for her as we went together into the Express office, where daily for weeks some fifty of the coffined dead were sent home,—"the sad place my boy used to bring his little bit of money to send me and children, and now must be brought home dead!"

Ah, it is well for us all to pause, and to think of what an awful sacrifice ourselves in our country were then and there redeemed! The old pole stand in the centre of the Diamond, around which for one month, beginning from the time of the battle, at eight o'clock in the morning, we were wont to collect with stores and with the arrival of teams to convey us to the battle-field and the temporary tent hospitals. Those weary mornings, hot and dusty with their tedious delays, their energetic efforts to supply ourselves with a sufficient load of needful articles for the wounded in our respective charges.

All have passed away, and with them the rich and abundant opportunities for usefulness to those illustrious heroes. Good God, how many thousands of those to whom we once ministered during our month sojourn are now sleeping in bloody graves, whose eternal silence the archangels trumpet alone can break. The photographs in Tyson's gallery seemed to speak of those times. It is decorated with flags and gaily lighted, while the band plays beneath its windows, but the pictures on the wall bring before us Culps and Granite Hill, where the slaughter was most terrific, the almost impregnable summit of Round Top, with its rocky batteries, on which many an unburied form now reposes, the Headquarters of the General commanding on the Taneytown road pierced with screaming shells on that awful day. The plainest and smallest of houses through his kitchen windows we gazed to-day, and whose undaunted and forever illustrious tenant urged "every man to do his duty and leave the result to all wise Providence." History will record how nobly this pledge was redeemed; even should history be silent, the graves to be consecrated to-morrow will be eloquent indeed. Cemetery Hill is here, with the breast-works crossing the pike in front, and its rounded arched gateway perforated with balls, the Cemetery itself, on which at noon on Friday, one hundred and fifty guns opened from rebel batteries, replied to by the same number, until the very hills trembled under one of the most terrific cannonades the world has ever heard. We will tread the spot with awe, for here in the thickest of the fight, General Meade, in tones which must have thrilled all around him, said, "You must hold this position if it costs every man." Gettysburg village is here, with the Seminary afterwards crowded with wounded rebels.

We have visited the site of our old hospital, that of the second corps, viewed our old camping ground, the broken cans, bottles, and boxes, the little heap of ashes where our fire had been, past the refreshing rill by the roadside where we daily stopped to drink through the woods, at the foot of whose trees the springing oats dropped where the horses had fed, served to mark our way, by the rebel encampment with its role of graves, in one of which sleeps all that is mortal of the boy Samuel Parish, whose sought with such earnest longing to lay hold of a crucified Saviour in his dying moments, as he breathed his life away on a little heap of straw. At the entrance to the grove, our dead met our eye each morning, wrapped in their blankets awaiting burial. Truly this ground has already been consecrated by the very extremity of human suffering; the amputating tents are gone, pitched elsewhere, the woods once resounding with shrieks are silent now, but the agony once endured, the buried limbs and bodies call to heaven for judgment on the authors of this rebellion. And a little beyond on one of the loveliest spots of all this field, on a hill overlooking the curious windings of the stream, far below at the foot of the tree I read, "Lieutenant Prestgraves, 7th Virginia." The affection of a brother had marked the spot and shielded it with stones. Laid with hundreds of others, fresh from the amputation table on the damp earth, this deluded, erring, and yet noble Christian met the king of terrors with such rapture as is granted to few.

As I read to him,

"There is a fountain filled with blood,"

and then bade him farewell, his eye lighted; he placed his hand for a moment on his breast, and then pointed upward; earth here, with its scenes of blood and carnage, heaven beyond, with its angels throng, composed of the redeemed martyrs and believers of all ages. Truly marvelous was the contrast. ✟

George A. Peltz,

Two Brass Buttons

A Story of the Christian Commission

✣ ✣ ✣ ✣ ✣ ✣ ✣

George Alexander Peltz

T
HE STORY, "Two Brass Buttons," first appeared in the *Philadelphia Weekly Press* on March 2, 1887. Two weeks later, the *Gettysburg Compiler* reprinted the heart-rending tale, opening the door to two mysteries.

The first mystery is the identity of the author. Although published under the name H. S. Peltz, it is undoubtedly the work of Reverend George Alexander Peltz. Born in Philadelphia in 1833, Peltz attended Lewisburg College. Following graduation in 1857, he pastored a mission church in New York City, later organized as Pilgrim Baptist Church. He remained there for eight years. In 1863, on leave from this church, Peltz served as a delegate of the United States Christian Commission.

After the Civil War, he embarked on a long and distinguished ministerial career. In October 1865 Peltz moved to Philadelphia to become pastor of the Tabernacle Baptist Church. Other pastorates included the South Baptist Church of Newark, N. J., and the First Baptist Church of Jamestown, N. Y.

Peltz dedicated much of his life to Sunday School work, traveling extensively throughout the eastern United States. He chaired the Baptist National Sunday-School Convention in St. Louis in 1869 and presided over the First International Sunday School Convention, held in Baltimore in 1875. He served as a member of the Convention Executive Committee for ten years. In 1876 he assumed the associate editorship of *The Sunday-School Times*, and later edited *The Baptist Teacher for Sunday-school Workers*.

Peltz was a prolific writer, contributing articles to the leading Sunday-school papers. His stories were collected for publication, including *Grandpa's Stories, or Home Talks Out of the Wonderful Book* (Philadelphia: Hubbard Brothers, 1885). He also edited *The Housewife's Library* (Philadelphia: Hubbard Brothers, 1883).

The second mystery of the story lies in its accuracy. Soon after its publication, a reporter for the *Gettysburg Compiler* discovered several minor discrepancies between Peltz' narrative and the actual events. For example, Dr. J. W. C. O'Neal, not Dr. Kneeland, kept detailed records of burial sites at Gettysburg, assisted by Tom McCullough, not Sam.

When the *Compiler* reporter reviewed Dr. O'Neal's notes, he found a reference to "Lieut. Donald Gordon, 28th Georgia, second corps ground, Schwartz's, back of barn." An additional entry placed Gordon's body next to George Briggs of Florida. However, the Twenty-eighth Georgia was not at Gettysburg. The Forty-eighth Georgia fought in the general vicinity, yet the roster shows no soldiers named Gordon or Spaulding. If Peltz had the unit name correct, it might have been the Columbus City Light Guard (Company A, Second Independent Battalion) or the Columbus Guards (Company C, Second Georgia Infantry), yet the names of Gordon or a Spaulding do not appear on the rosters of those units. The name of George Briggs is not found on any rosters of Florida troops at Gettysburg. In addition, Dr. O'Neal's original listing of gravesites fails to list those names. There are two explanations. It is possible that Doctor O'Neal added the names after Peltz, Mr. Gordon, and the Doctor recovered the bodies. It is also plausible that O'Neal "doctored" his records after reading the story.

Did Peltz embellish the story or make it up? Did he simply tell a true story but change the names? Katherine Georg Harrison, chief historian at Gettysburg National Military Park, concluded, "The whole story is screwy and may be either made up completely as a historical novel, or else the good pastor's memory was totally faulty as to all names and units." Yet, the narrative contains just enough truth to make it compelling, especially its description of the barn and its Confederate wounded in the Second Corps Hospital. The story's narrator has a crucial meeting on a steamer as he returns from presiding over a religious convention in Mobile, Alabama, eight years after Gettysburg – a role that Peltz often filled, although Charleston, South Carolina, hosted the major Baptist Sunday School convention of 1871.

Peltz specialized in turning Biblical stories into readable moral tales, and, one suspects, used his talents to turn his wartime experience into a wonderful dramatic sketch. The tale illustrates the growing bonds between North and South, twenty-five years after the last shot at Gettysburg.[1] ✢

[2] Kathyrn Georg Harrison, Memo, Gettysburg National Park research files.

IN THE SUNNY CORNER of my study stands a quaint, old-fashioned cabinet. While rummaging aimlessly through its cedar recesses not long ago I came upon a lot of relics from the battle-field of Gettysburg. There was a handful of bullets battered into curious shapes, a grapeshot and the fragment of a shell cut from the stump of a tree on the crest of Culp's Hill. Taking up a musty piece of leather shaped like a crescent, I poked my finger through a ragged hole in its centre. It was the visor cut from the cap of a Pennsylvania volunteer, and the ragged hole was torn by the rifle ball that pierced his brain. And down in the corner of the lower drawer my eyes fell upon a sealed envelope. I brushed away the dust and read upon its time-stained surface the inscription:

Donald Gordon

Twenty-Eighth Georgia

C.S.A., July 13, 1863–July 13, 1871.

I broke the seal—reverently, not carelessly—and there fell into my hands two brass buttons. They were tarnished and spotted with verdigris, for they had been eight years under ground before they reached my cabinet. But still bright on the blackened background shone the raised shield and the letters C.S.A.—the initials of an empty name, the heraldry of a lost cause. No common place relics, these. The buttons had a story.

In the Spring of 1863 I was the young pastor of a new but rapidly growing mission in New York City. Scarcely a day that brought its budget of battle news but brought bereavement to some one who had the right to look to me for comfort and protection. Yet I longed with the longing of youth for work that was nearer the front. At last the opportunity came. On the night of the 30th of June, 1863, my church voted me a month's vacation. Twenty-four hours later I had determined how and where I would spend it, for the telegraph had thrilled the pulse of the North with the ominous news of the first day's fight at Gettysburg.

The first relief train that left the City of Brotherly Love for the field where brothers had met in deadly hate bore a hundred Good Samaritans all bent upon the same errand and each, like myself, wearing upon his breast the silver scroll badge of the United States Christian Commission.

On the sultriest of July's sultry days I entered the little town of Gettysburg and found the borough transformed into one great hospital. Every building of considerable proportions—courthouse, church and store—was an improvised hospital ward crowded to suffocation with men in every stage of mortal agony. Even the public square in the centre of the village was filled with mangled forms. There they lay, poor fellows, their heads pillowed on the sun-baked ground, unsheltered from the burning heat of Midsummer, suffering, groaning, dying. There were not surgeons enough to care for half of those who sorely needed their skill. There were not homes enough to shelter half of those who were dying for lack of the commonest comforts. Confusion reigned everywhere. In the garish red brick warehouse fronting the square on the West, wherein the Christian Commission had established headquarters, I presented my credentials and was assigned to duty in a portion of the field hospital of the Second Corps.

A drive of half an hour down the old Baltimore Pike, between fields robbed of all their fences, trodden down by troops and strewn with the debris of an army, a turn to the right and across Rock Creek by a shallow ford brought me to my destination. The Wertz farm lay just East of the clump of woods wherein the Second Army Corps had established its surgical and medical headquarters—a position naturally selected by reason of the bountiful supply of water afforded by Rock Creek and the comparative proximity of the wooded patch to the lines where the Second Corps had done its fighting on July 3. The old farmhouse was only one of a half dozen occupied by the men of Hancock's corps, but it was a type of them all. Its every room was a chamber of death and the boards of the shambling porch that girdled it were stained with the blood of the men for whom there was no room inside. The shade of a vine-clad trellis gave these poor fellows partial shelter from the scorching heat. West of the farmhouse, and only a stone's throw from the vine-clad porch with its freight of human misery, stood the old barn. This was devoted exclusively to the wounded of the Confederate army, and while the soldiers of the North were dying for lack of care it was not strange that these poor strangers were left in an even worse condition. Yet they had not been wholly neglected, for the grim sight of the rudely constructed table just outside the barn doors, and a pair of surgeons working above it with their arms bared to the elbows, told me that Science, with her knives and opiates, was already doing her merciful work. It was to the barn that I was assigned, to co-operate with the surgeons as chief nurse.

Within the cramped quarters of that barn were eighty men, all terribly wounded. It was a barn of a type common in Adams County—and, indeed, everywhere—the main entrance approached by an inclined driveway, the threshing-floor in the middle flanked on either side by the hay-lofts, and beneath the threshing-floor the cattle pens opening upon the barnyard in the rear. The smaller of the barn doors had been unhinged to serve as surgeon's tables, and there on the threshing floor and haylofts of peaceful husbandry, war had garnered its awful harvest of death and agony. Such a harvest no Pennsylvania barn ever stored before or since. Every available inch of space was occupied. The men lay close to each other, side by side in long rows, as compactly as when a few days before, in full vigor of manhood, they marched shoulder to shoulder across the Emmettsburg Road, undaunted by the grape and canister from eighty Union guns, as compactly as we laid their mangled bodies a few days later, shoulder to shoulder in the long trenches of the stubble-field. The cattle-pens, too, still reeking with the litter of the barnyard, were as densely packed with victims as the threshing-floor above, and I noticed with horror, as I assisted at the dressing of a bleeding wound, that the blood of the patient filtered through the cracks and knot-holes of the floor and dripped upon the sufferers below.

As night came on, darkness threw a kindly mantle over such repulsive sights, but the horror of the situation was hardly less acute. The only illumi-nation of the place came from the sickly yellow glow of an army lantern. A square box-like contrivance hung from a joist, with an oil lamp in the middle and four cracked panes of glass, so soiled that the dull yellow rays barely struggled through them. The men—restless, suffering and unable to sleep—tossed and moaned and raved in wild delirium. The weather-beaten barn resounded with a horrid chorus of curses, imprecations, and groans that sounded doubly awful at dead of night, and the old army lantern's glimmering light wrought weird, fantastic shadows among the cobwebbed rafters of the roof.

II.

IT WAS IN THIS CHAMBER OF HORRORS and on the first night of my appren-ticeship as a Good Samaritan that I met Donald Gordon of the 28th Georgia. I saw the gleam of a lantern outside the barn, and a rough but kindly voice said: "Take him in here, boys." Then the lantern flashed momentarily on the grim relics of the surgeon's table near the doorway, there was a shuffling of feet upon the threshold and two men entered and deposited a stretcher upon the floor. Behind them came a third, who wore his left arm in a sling rudely improvised from a cartridge belt and a handkerchief. The two who were able-bodied cleared a spot by removing the body of a poor fellow who had just breathed his last. The corpse was taken outside to be buried in the morning, and then Donald Gordon was lifted tenderly from the stretcher and placed in the spot where the dead man had lain.

In the flickering light of the lantern I saw his face, handsome, though pale and haggard from suffering. It was the face of a young man—he was barely 20—and every feature was an index of manliness, graced with the highest culture and refinement.

Lieutenant Gordon was—to use in its best sense a phrase that has sometimes been abused—a Southern gentleman. Between him and his faithful comrade, Tom Spaulding, the wounded soldier whose rough but kindly voice had directed the bearers of the stretcher where to lay their burden, there existed that peculiar type of affection that is not uncommon between men of widely opposite attainments. Gordon was the son of a moderately wealthy manufacturer of Columbus, Georgia. He had graduated from college with distinction, and when the war broke out, though he had just completed his course in a theological seminary, he enlisted with the members of the Columbus Light Guard in the 28th Georgia. Spaulding, who was a sergeant in the same company, was a big-hearted fellow of noble impulses, but not a man of brilliant parts. It was a schoolboy friendship begun in the schools of Columbus and never outgrown by either, though the one had far outstripped the other in scholarship and social rank. The Lieutenant was wounded dangerously. A grape shot—one of the drops in the iron storm hurled from Hancock's guns—had struck and shattered his right leg just above the knee. The Sergeant's wounded arm, painful but not serious, did not prevent the many acts of ministering kindness that proved his loyal devotion to his comrade. Early in the day following that first wretched night in the barn hospital Donald Gordon's shattered limb was amputated, but he never rallied from the shock. He sank steadily day by day and when the dawn of July 12 lighted up the gloomy corners of the old barn it was plain that before another sunrise came the struggle would be over. Gordon knew the end was near and awaited it with patient courage. Tom Spaulding, kneeling beside him, pressed his hand and asked gently what he could do to cheer him. From force of military habit the subaltern had addressed his friend as "Lieutenant."

"Drop the Lieutenant, Tom," said Gordon, with a faint smile, "We're both off duty now. Call me Don, as you used to when we were in school together."

Then his eyes closed and he was silent for a time. When the big brown eyes opened again and looked vacantly toward the grimy rafters of the barn, it was clear that the soldier's mind was clouded slightly by the raging fever that had racked his body for forty-eight hours.

"Don, old fellow, do you want anything?" whispered Spaulding.

"Yes," he faltered. "Tom, I—I want to be dressed," and then with a struggle to make his meaning clear, he went on faintly, "Tom, you I know I've lived like a gentleman. I know it's hard to do much but I think I'd feel better if you could wash my face and cool my hands." Then, after a pause, he went on. "And Tom, can't you dress me in a clean shirt? I—I don't feel clean. You know, old fellow, I've lived like a gentleman, and—well, I want to—to die like a gentleman."

Tenderly as men could, we sponged the fevered body with tepid water and dressed the dying soldier in some neat linen taken from the hospital stores. His face expressed the gratitude he was too weak to speak but as he sank back upon the blanket that served as a rude pillow, he noticed the two little cameo studs that still remained screwed into the soiled shirt front.

"Put in the studs, too," he said. "Mother gave me those. Let me keep them until—until I go home again." We did as he bade us and then, apparently satisfied, he sank into a quiet sleep. Toward evening he roused again. Spaulding was still beside him, but my duties for the time had called me elsewhere. His sleep had apparently given the dying man a momentary lease of new strength, and for half an hour he talked with his comrade in whispers as the two lay side by side. It was then that he entrusted to Tom Spaulding his last messages.

What passed between the men at that time I do not know and if I did, the sacred confidences of that last half hour should remain inviolate. I only know that sundry little trinkets—among them a ring, the gift of his father, and a medallion locket enclosing a portrait of the woman who hoped to be his wife—passed from the hands of the dying Lieutenant to those of the Sergeant who still hoped to see friends and home again. Shortly before midnight I joined them and remained until the end. I asked the young officer if there was aught I could do for him.

"Nothing, pastor," he answered. (It was a fancy of his to call me pastor.) "Nothing, Tom has taken all the messages I want to send. He will see to everything. You've been very kind, pastor. I thank you." He hesitated a moment and then added, "Yes, only one thing—do the best you can to give me a Christian burial." Then, turning from me to his comrade, he faltered: "And you, Tom, when you can—when the war is over—take me back to mother and Mattie." Then the weary eyelids drooped, the soldier fell into a painless stupor and just as the sickly glow of the old army lantern began to pale in the coming dawn of another sultry day, Donald Gordon died.

The sun was beating down upon the trench in the stubble-field when we carried the body out for burial. All that was possible had been done to give the dead Lieutenant the Christian burial he craved. The wasted form was wrapped closely in a blanket and about the soldier's head and face I tied his military jacket, fastening the sleeves around his neck. Then the little funeral party started from the barn toward the trenches. Two of the mourners, a Confederate prisoner and myself, carried the body, one at either end of the stretcher on which the wounded soldier had entered the barn a week before. The third, Tom Spaulding, walked silently beside it with downcast head. We had not far to go. Following the well-beaten path through the barn yard and across a rustic bridge that spanned a small rivulet, we entered the stubble-field and tramped on, a hundred yards perhaps, to the open end of the second of two parallel trenches. There we did what little we could to make a Christian burial. From the sides of a pair of cracker boxes, framed over and around the body as it lay in the trench, we improvised the best substitute for a coffin that the exigencies of war would permit. Then from memory, I spoke a short burial service, offered a brief prayer, while the faithful Spaulding knelt beside me with uncovered head, and, with the terse but solemn formula, "Dust to dust, ashes to ashes," committed the body of Donald Gordon to the earth of the battle-field whereon he fell. On his right, as he lay in the shallow trench, slept 100 men who died for the same lost cause—next to him the herculean frame of John Briggs, a Florida soldier, who gave up the struggle only twenty minutes after the Lieutenant died and was buried an hour before him. On his left, in the same serried ranks of the fallen, we had laid, before I left the wretched barn forever, 200 more of the Army of Northern Virginia.

Through all the later hours of that funeral day, Tom Spaulding sat, knife in hand, patiently carving letters in the lid of a box that I had nailed to the threshold of the barn so that he might work upon it with his one uncrippled arm. In the evening he showed me his work. Deep in the yielding pine he had cut his simple epitaph: "Lieutenant Don Gordon, 28th Georgia, C.S.A." He pointed significantly toward the stubble-field as he explained briefly:

"Shingles with a name written on them hurriedly won't stand the weather long. This will do better, I think." So the next day we drove the board deep into the ground at the head of the spot where Donald Gordon lay and left it there—an humble monument to mark a soldier's grave.

Three weeks longer I toiled on amid the ghastly scenes of the barn hospital, and when at last I kissed my wife and babies at home again I had a little battle of my own to fight—six weeks' tussle with malignant typhoid fever.

Years afterwards I learned that the tender messages entrusted to the Sergeant, the ring, the medallion and the portrait, never reached the dear ones in Columbus and they heard not a word of how Don Gordon died. Poor, faithful Tom Spaulding's fate was even more terrible than his comrade's. He recovered from his wound, was exchanged soon after, rejoined the Army of Northern Virginia and was shot dead in the disastrous attack at Mine Run. Had I known this at the time my story might not be worth telling, for I might have done, in part at least, what Donald Gordon left him to do. But I did not know it. And so for eight years Donald Gordon slept beneath the field of Gettysburg, while his comrade's body lay I know not where. I only know that somewhere in the battle-scarred South—on the field where he fell, or in some soldiers' cemetery, perchance—Tom Spaulding's body lies, an insignificant unit in the great unnumbered army of the unknown dead.

III.

ONE PLEASANT EVENING in July, eight years after the battle of Gettysburg, the passenger steamer Oriole was making her night trip Northward over the waters of Mobile Bay. Wearied by the task of presiding for three days over a religious convention and glad to be again on my way home, I had sought the hurricane deck and dropped into a comfortable canvas easy chair to rest. I had long since ceased to harrow my soul with the recollections of those awful days in the old barn hospital. I don't know why it was, therefore, that on that particular night my thoughts persistently reverted to that funeral scene by the trench in the stubble-field and Tom Spaulding's headboard with its simple epitaph. Perhaps it was only the coincidence of time, coupled with the sense of being beneath Southern skies, that recalled the memory of the Southern soldier.

Abandoned to my own musings, I sat there watching the wondrous play of phosphorescent light in the steamer's wake and quite unconscious of the presence of the portly middle-aged gentleman who sat opposite me on the starboard side, and was the only other occupant of that part of the deck. His abortive efforts to strike a match and a mildly impatient exclamation at his failure reminded me that I had a neighbor in distress. I was about to rise and offer him a light when he came toward me. "Thank you, sir," he said, pleasantly, as he drew the first puff from his mild Key West. "I seem to have lost my old-time knack of striking fire in a breeze." Then, as he glanced at my face for the first time, he smiled and extended his hand in greeting.

"Why, Doctor, glad to see you. I didn't know you were aboard. Pardon me for introducing myself. You don't know me, but I heard your address last evening in Mobile." As he spoke he was fumbling in his wallet and producing a card, he handed it to me and bowed slightly. Then, comprehending that it was too dark to read it, he added: "My name is Charles P. Winthrop, sir, of Columbus—Columbus, Georgia." We sat down together and chatted a while when the late convention and its doings, and then when the conversation seemed likely to flag I did what a chance acquaintance always does who has little to guide him save the name of the town one hails from. I sought to name some mutual friend. I might have named a Christian minister of Columbus whom I knew quite well; but somehow the instant the middle-aged gentleman said "of Columbus—Columbus, Georgia," I had seen again in memory that pine headboard, with its carved inscription, "Lieutenant Don Gordon, 28th Georgia, C.S.A." And so I simply followed my first impulse when I said:

"Do you happen to know a family in your town named Gordon; had a son, a splendid young fellow, killed in the war?"

"Gordon? Caleb Gordon? Why, yes, I know the old gentleman well, sir. A neighbor of mine, in fact, and a member of the same church." Mr. Winthrop was affable. He was evidently pleased that my mental grappling for a mutual friend had been so fortunate in its very first venture, and his face was beaming with gratification as he added: "You know Caleb Gordon, then! Fine old gentleman, sir; true as steel and gentle as a woman; generous, too, generous to a fault."

"No," I said quietly, and with a touch of sadness, "I don't know the father, but I knew the son."

"Don, was it? Yes, yes, poor Don! That was a sad blow to the old gentleman, and isn't it strange, sir, with all the money and time Caleb Gordon has spent to get all the facts, that he never learned the first word of how poor Don died, or where he was buried. That seems to be the saddest part of it, sir; don't you think so? Lost! Simply lost to them and not a soul knows the facts! Many such cases during the war, no doubt, all through the — "

Mr. Winthrop stopped and looked up in my face. I had dropped my cigar to the deck. The half desultory interest I had shown in the conversation was gone and I was looking eagerly into his eyes, my voice shaking with suppressed emotion as I said: "Stop a moment. Did you say Donald Gordon's body was never recovered?"

"Never recovered? Why, sir, there's not a clue—but what's the matter, sir, are you ill?"

"No, go on; tell me all about it," I said, struggling to regain my composure. "But I'll tell you why I'm surprised," I added curbing my eagerness. "It is because—because I can recover that body for I buried it with my own hands."

It was now Mr. Winthrop's turn to be surprised, and he studied my face incredulously a moment almost as though he mistrusted me. I told him the facts briefly and then he explained to me how Caleb Gordon had only heard that his son had fallen at Gettysburg, how he had vainly exhausted every possible means of learning further details, and still clung to the fond hope of some day recovering the body.

An hour later Mr. Winthrop and myself parted. I never saw him again. He took the train for Columbus, and I continued my journey North. I am a fairly good traveler, and I had a "Middle-lower" berth, but I did not sleep well. I was restless, and when at last I fell into a troubled slumber my dreams were haunted by the horrors of the field hospital at Gettysburg, and the rumble of the cars seemed to my fevered brain the groans of dying men.

IV.

ON THE THIRD DAY after my return to Philadelphia the servant brought to my study a card bearing the name of Caleb Gordon. He had come from Columbus to recover the lost body of his son. The old gentleman was impatient, eager to leave for the field at once. I was anxious to help him and hopeful of success, I canceled some engagements, postponed others, and in forty-eight hours was again on the way to Gettysburg with Donald Gordon's father beside me. During the first stage of the journey he had drawn from me eagerly every detail of his son's death and burial, every little incident I could remember of his last hours of life. After that the father relapsed into silent brooding, but as I watched his face I knew that the hope of an old man's life must be realized or blighted by the outcome of that strange journey.

We stopped in the borough of Gettysburg only long enough to enlist the services of two helpers—one of them Dr. Kneeland, an elderly physician, who had made a study of the burial trenches and had thereby been instrumental in recovering many bodies; the other, the Doctor's negro driver, who was equipped with a spade and a long, narrow box. Then we drove together down the old Baltimore pike. The scene was a perfect picture of peace and thrifty industry. I never realized before what a wonderful difference so significant an element as the presence or absence of a lot of crazy fences makes in the ensemble of a landscape. Until we had forded Rock Creek at the same shallow ford and approached the old farmhouse, it seemed to me almost like a strange country we were traversing. But there at last was the same shambling porch where I first saw the long lines of wounded and dying men and the same vine-clad trellis that sheltered them from the cruel heat. The crimson hollyhocks in the dooryard were blooming in all their splendor—just as they bloomed eight years before. It was the 13th of July eight years to a day since Donald Gordon died. It was the same place, and yet it was not the same place. My first bitter disappointment came when I learned that there was not a soul in that house who could help us accomplish our purpose, for the Wertz farm had passed into other hands.

I walked around the corner of the vine-covered porch expecting to see the familiar old barn. The barn had vanished too. The absence of the barn confused me, but I walked after the Doctor as he followed the direction indicated by his memoranda. It was not hard to locate where the stubble-field had been, for it was a spacious tract of many acres, but to locate the precise line of the trenches was a far more delicate task. The stubble-field, moreover, was a stubble-field no longer. It was waving high with corn. The Doctor paused in the labyrinth of little cornhills. "According to my notion," he said, "the trenches ran right along here, about thirty feet from the present fence line."

"I think you are wrong," I returned. "We've not gone far enough."

"Well, we can soon test that," he answered. Then at his direction the negro struck his spade into the soil between two hills of corn. As he dug down beneath the superficial stratum it was plain to his practised eye that the subsoil had never been disturbed. I could see that the Doctor was discouraged by his failure, though not greatly surprised by it. Upon some pretext he called me apart from Caleb Gordon, who had been an eager spectator of the test, and then he said to me in whispers: "This thing, I fear, is hopeless. It was a foolish thing for the gentleman to come a thousand miles on a errand like this. You see yourself it's like hunting a needle in a haystack, and if we strike the line and find a body, how can we know it's the right one? It's hard, very hard, but really, I think you'd better try and discourage him and let him down easy, so to speak. A single body in a wilderness of corn stalks! The thing is almost impossible."

"Discourage him?" I answered. "I can not do that. I haven't the courage."

"Then I must," said the Doctor, and in spite of my exhortations not to give up so soon, he called to Caleb Gordon and told him what he had just told me. The old man's face grew pale, but the lines of his mouth were firmly drawn. This was his resolute reply:

"I am not a wealthy man, Doctor, but I have money enough to buy this farm. My wife knows that I am here today. If I go home without what I came for it will break her heart. Before I admit that this task is hopeless I will buy this place and dig over inch by inch until I find the body of my son."

The Doctor flushed at the father's answer, but I saw that if we were to succeed it must be by reliance upon myself rather than upon my colleague.

"Wait here for me," I said, and started again toward the farmhouse. As I emerged from the labyrinth of corn and looked toward the clover field beyond it, I noticed something significant that had escaped out observation. Across the even surface of the clover field ran two parallel and well-defined lines like ground swells on the surface of the sea. Along those lines the clover was waving almost knee-deep in a rich dark-green, in sharp contrast with the sparse and ragged growth elsewhere. Those were the lines of the trenches.

If I could produce those lines into the cornfield and then determine the point where they ended I might yet succeed. With such aid as the matter-of-fact young farmer was able to give, I located as nearly as possible the site of the old barn, keeping all the while in my mind's eye the relative position of those billowy lines in the clover field beyond. Then I banished every other thought, concentrating all my faculties upon the task of recalling the past.

I started from the vacant site of the old barn hospital and paced slowly like one walking in a trance. Once more I was trudging at the end of a stretcher with the body of a dead soldier. My mind obliterated eight years and I was again carrying the body of Donald Gordon out for burial in the blaze of the midday sun. I crossed the dry bed of the rivulet, guessing at the point where the rustic bridge had stood. I was only half-conscious then of the direction I took, but from the moment I crossed the parched stones in the bed of the brook I began counting my steps. Pacing slowly forward with my head bent toward the ground I hardly knew I had struck into the cornfield again until I had scaled the fence and was impatiently brushing aside the tasseled stalks that cumbered my path. When at last I stopped, I know not why I stopped, I only followed an uncontrollable impulse. I could not have told how far I had gone, but felt that it was just as far as I had gone eight years ago that morning, and, when my friends came hurrying toward me in response to my shout, it was in a tone of confidence that I said:

"The body of Donald Gordon lies within ten paces of where I now stand."

Dr. Kneeland said I was surely wrong; the trenches lay closer to the fence line. "Let the spade test that," I replied, as I motioned to the negro to dig. He dug out one hill of corn ten feet from where I stood, struck down a foot or two beneath the surface and found nothing.

"Come closer to me and try again," I said. He laid another corn stalk aside the first and struck his spade almost at my feet. We stood in painful silence watching each spadeful of earth tossed out beside us. Ten inches below the surface the ground suddenly crumbled in spots and caved into the hole.

"That settles it," exclaimed the Doctor. "We're on the line of the trench." Stopping only to grasp my hand warmly, he added: "Now, Sam, go carefully." Sam turned up three more spadefuls of loose loam while Caleb Gordon bent his silvered head above the negro, intent upon his every motion. In the third spadeful of loam Sam turned up something else—something long and hard with knobs at the ends.

"Stop," said the Doctor. He sprang forward, grasped the relic and brushed away the soil that clung to a human bone. He studied it carefully a moment with a sort of professional zest, soliloquizing thus as he brushed it clean and eyed its proportions: "A thigh bone, the thigh bone of an unusually tall man; see how long it is. That man must have stood over six feet if he was well proportioned." Then his keen eye caught another peculiarity. "Ah, see that," he added; pointing to a ragged break in the knob that once made part of the hip joint. "This is a fractured thigh bone; a tall man struck by a shot just below the hip." Oh, what a world of meaning that diagnosis had for me. It told me that Caleb Gordon's hope would not be blighted. "That," said I, "is the thigh bone of John Briggs, a Florida soldier."

The Doctor smiled incredulously. "And how on earth do you know that?"

"I know it," I replied, "because John Briggs, a great muscular fellow, who stood six feet four, was the one and only man who died in the barn hospital from a fractured leg who had not previously had that leg amputated. He was struck so high up, and the hip was so shattered that amputation was impossible."

"Well, I must admit that looks plausible," said the Doctor contemplatively, picking the loam out of the ragged fracture with the blade of his knife. "Now, if you could only remember when this Briggs died.—"

"Exactly," I interrupted. "He and Donald Gordon died the same night and Gordon lies right there beside him, for the two were buried within an hour."

"Thank God!" exclaimed Caleb Gordon, and the old man, for the first time in all the trying ordeal, broke down and wept like a child, with his arms about my neck. But he was too eager now to yield to his emotions long. Sam was digging again, fifteen inches to the right of where we found the thigh bone of John Briggs. Two more corn-stalks had been uprooted, and the father of Lieutenant Gordon was down on his knees in the corn-field, peering into the deepening hole and listening to the dull grating of the negro's spade. A few minutes of patient digging and Sam turned up the rotten fragments of a board. Then, with careful hands, we removed one by one the decayed splinters of the cracker box from which that rude coffin was improvised eight years before, and gradually uncovered the whole length of the body. The dank, mouldy shreds of the blanket and the army jacket that shrouded the soldier's form dropped to pieces as we touched them, but six brass buttons with the letters C.S.A. stamped upon the shield dropped from the damp shreds of the jacket, and Caleb Gordon seized them like a man who has found a precious treasure. Then one by one the bones of Lieutenant Gordon's body were lifted from their grave and laid each in its proper place upon the ground, until there was not a fragment missing save the lower part of the right leg that was severed by the amputation.

Caleb Gordon stooped again and took in his hands the skull of his son. For a moment the old man's eyes gazed into the sightless sockets of his first born; his hands caressed the smooth frontal bones of the well-rounded forehead and then he carefully examined the perfect rows of teeth still firm and white.

"It is he," he faltered, "I would know my boy's forehead anywhere. Yes, there can be no doubt. See, even the teeth complete the evidence. These gold two fillings were the only imperfections."

While the old man stood fingering the skull and pointing out, between his sobs, each evidence of identity, the Doctor, who had been searching in the shreds of the rotten blanket that dropped from the dead man's ribs, made a discovery that removed the last possible shadow of a doubt. "There is something that perhaps you will value," he said, and he placed in Caleb Gordon's outstretched hand a little cameo shirt stud.

Our task was done. The identity was established beyond peradventure. Caleb Gordon's hope was realized. We had disturbed just four hills of corn.

It was well that we succeeded when we did. A few months later the task would have been hopeless, for within a year the state of Virginia made an appropriation and every Confederate body still unclaimed was disinterred and buried in the great soldier's cemetery of Richmond.

V.

ONE MORE SCENE and this sombre sketch is finished. This, too, is a funeral scene, but not like that other in the stubble-field. At Donald Gordon's second burial the bright sunshine of the South flashed upon the radiant shafts of marble and polished granite in the beautiful little cemetery of Columbus. That second sepulture was marked by such reverent ministrations as became the memory of a Christian and such martial honors as were due the fame of a soldier. The survivors of the Columbus Light Guard were there to do their part. Their muskets spoke the martial requiem over their comrade's tomb, and as the smoke over the funeral volley cleared away two women stood by Donald Gordon's grave weeping tears of mingled joy and sorrow. The one, careworn and silver-haired, was his mother; the other, still young, a queenly Southern woman, with hair as black as the crape veil that touched it, was in all but name his widow. And as they turned away at last, the silver-haired mother smiled sweetly as she spoke:

"We should be thankful, Mattie, very thankful," she said, "for at last we have poor Don at home again."

This is the story that came to me so vividly as I sat by my quaint old secretary and polished back to brightness the two brass buttons that Caleb Gordon had given me from his store of treasures. It was not much that I had done. Chance—or perhaps I should say Providence—had done far more than I. And yet as I sat there in my quiet study and thought it all over, I was conscious of a sweet sense of satisfaction as rare as it is exquisite. I did not stop to analyze the feeling; but perhaps it was because I had at least been instrumental in fulfilling the last two injunctions of a dying man. Donald Gordon had at last received a Christian burial, and to-day he sleeps beneath a bower of roses planted by the loving lands of mother and Mattie. ✛